Words of Power

This excellent study provides a fresh and intriguing approach to the cultural status of what Jem Bloomfield calls "Shakespeare and the Bible". Engagingly written and full of surprising insights, *Words of Power* argues for the overlap between how these texts are approached in both popular and scholarly culture. Bloomfield takes concepts from biblical scholarship – such as "canon" and the "scriptural" mode of reading (which presuppose that the text says nothing trivial) – and fruitfully explores how they can be used to challenge preconceptions about the way that both Shakespeare and the Bible should be read.

Beatrice Groves, Research Lecturer
in Renaissance Literature, University of Oxford

Jem Bloomfield's lively study asks what it means to put faith in a book. It unpicks the historical contingency of both the Bible and Shakespeare's Complete Works, and demonstrates that the more interesting question is not what these books *are*, but what they *are needed to be*. By highlighting the role played by tradition, assumption and worldview in shaping reading practices, Bloomfield makes an important call for critical awareness of how words, both sacred and secular, gain their power.

Peter Kirwan, Assistant Professor in Shakespeare
and Early Modern Drama, University of Nottingham

Jem Bloomfield is thunderously successful in stimulating readers to look in fresh ways at these twin peaks of English literary culture. This short book is not only a book about the Bible and Shakespeare, but on the nature of texts in general: how they are formed and performed, how they become "sacred", how they form communities and function within cultures, and how they can help us to appreciate the "remarkable strangeness" of both the past and the present.

John Halton, blogger at Curlew River

Words of Power

Reading Shakespeare and the Bible

Jem Bloomfield

The Lutterworth Press

The Lutterworth Press

P.O. Box 60
Cambridge
CB1 2NT
United Kingdom

www.lutterworth.com
publishing@lutterworth.com

ISBN: 978 0 7188 9413 9

British Library Cataloguing in Publication Data
A record is available from the British Library

First published by The Lutterworth Press, 2016

Contents

To my mother,
Diane Elizabeth Bloomfield,

and to the memory of my father,
Christopher Arthur Bloomfield.

Acknowledgements

This book is the product of a long process of learning and thinking, and it would be impossible to adequately thank everyone who contributed to the ideas presented here, whilst still bringing the manuscript in at a manageable length. However, some names stand out particularly, and I hope anyone I've left out will forgive me.

Thanks go to Peter McCullough and Karen Edwards, who both contributed to my interest in the Bible as an academic field without knowing it at the time. Pascale Aebischer and Jane Milling taught me an extraordinary amount about Shakespeare and Performance Studies, as well as showing me how academic life worked and how to get from talking excitedly for hours to producing a coherent collection of pages.

Peter Kirwan has been an unfailingly kind colleague, always willing to share his ideas and to tactfully suggest where mine could be improved. I would also like to thank Lucie Sutherland, Julie Sanders, Nicola Royan, Christina Lee and the other members of the School of English, who make the University of Nottingham such a stimulating place to work.

The clergy and congregation of St. Mary Magdalen in Oxford provided a supportive and invigorating community where the ideas in this book first developed, and I'm grateful as well to St. John the Baptist in Beeston, where we moved whilst I was writing it. Both churches nurture intellectual and creative engagement with the Bible in ways that this book reflects. The Shakespeare Institute at Stratford-upon-Avon (and its current director Michael Dobson) must take some of the blame also, for the place's repeated hospitality and the scholarly environment it provides to all sorts of people who aren't officially members.

Philip Law brought the book closer to existence, and once it was written Fiona Christie and Angharad Thomas at Lutterworth guided me through the process of editing and launching it. Sian Nielson,

Briony Frost and Lisa Stead helped with friendly support from their adjacent intellectual fields. This book would not have happened without Sheenagh, nor would so much else.

Introduction

We often find "the Bible and Shakespeare" grouped together in popular discussions, as if they form a central core of human (or at least Anglo-Saxon) civilisation. The long-running BBC radio programme *Desert Island Discs* famously asks celebrities what records they would want to take if they were being marooned alone, along with a single book and a luxury item to cheer their solitude and make the castaway life a bit more worth living. The only two books that guests are not permitted to choose are the Bible and the complete works of Shakespeare, since these are assumed to have been already deposited on the island by some enterprising (and vaguely heterodox) branch of the Gideon Society. Behind this stricture lies, perhaps, the assumption that so many celebrities would choose either one or other of these volumes that the programme would become tediously predictable. But there is also a suggestion, in the image of the castaway with their neatly bound copies of the Bible and Shakespeare, that these are the books that can provide a complete life in themselves, that they can either replace the society of other people, or provide the individual with the potted results of previous centuries of culture. Indeed, as I was working on this book, the National Secular Society started a campaign to persuade the BBC to remove this aspect of the programme, which was duly followed by a counterblast from right wing newspapers at the abandonment of "our Bible" and "our Christian culture".[1] Whatever practicalities of radio format caused the Bible to first appear on *Desert Island Discs*, its potential removal is seen – by both sides – as a statement about the beliefs of Anglophone culture.

There are a number of other possible echoes in the couplet of "the Bible and Shakespeare". They might be read as a *hendiadys*, the rhetorical device that Shakespeare himself frequently employed,

---

1. e.g. Allan Massie's column, "We Can't Cast Away Our Bible", *The Telegraph*, 11ᵗʰ August 2013.

and which brackets together two similar terms whose overlapping meanings cannot quite be distinguished from each other in the final phrase, such as "law and order" or "house and home". Particularly in the nineteenth century, "the Bible and Shakespeare" might be seen as a hendiadys, a joint repository of authority whose internal borders were somewhat blurry but whose external clout was tremendous. Or the two terms might mark out the two medieval spheres of power: the spiritual and temporal. Phrased slightly differently, they might designate two areas of knowledge or wisdom: the sacred and the secular. In Britain – given the importance of the Church of England and the King James Bible in the history of its politics and culture, as well as the enshrining of Shakespeare as the "national poet" – they might be read as the twin pillars of the establishment.

Sacred Texts?

The works of Shakespeare and the Bible are both "sacred texts" in their different ways.[1] I use that category not to suggest that they have equivalent value, or to make suggestions about the origins of their texts or their potential to affect people. I simply mean to point out the striking parallels in the ways they have been regarded and treated by certain groups. The Biblical critic John Barton defines "scriptural status" as a function of how a text is read. He identifies a number of related ways in which a book is treated distinctively by readers once it has been called "Scripture", focusing on the assumptions which this label brings *prior* to each individual reading. A Scripture is "a text that matters and which contains no trivialities, nothing ephemeral" (135). He gives the example of Paul's interpretation of Deuteronomy 25:4, "You shall not muzzle an ox while it is treading out the corn". Paul did not care about animal rights, and therefore read this as an

---

1. Throughout this book, I will be discussing the Bible and its reading within a specifically Christian tradition, and using the terms "New Testament" and "Old Testament" as designations of the way these collections of texts function in that tradition. I have not attempted to discuss the rich and varied traditions of Jewish interpretation of the same texts, except when these impinge obviously on the Christian reading. This is not intended in any way as a slight, or a suggestion that other interpretative traditions – especially those of Judaism – are wrong, but simply to define the scope of this particular book. In the chapters on textual criticism and the canon, I will also be focusing on the New Testament, as a collection of consciously Christian works that built on an existing set of Scriptures.

allegory for the right of religious teachers to be paid for the work they carry out. The other possibility – that the verse means nothing of importance – is ignored because of the book's scriptural status. In fact, Barton makes an explicit comparison with Shakespeare whilst proposing this idea, suggesting that in English literature there is "a taboo" against reading the books considered to be vaguely "scriptural" in a way that assumes them to be trivial (135).

> It is not acceptable to think Shakespeare is deeply uninteresting, that he wrote on silly and boring themes, that his plots are inconsequential. And if such thoughts do strike the reader, the "canonical" status of Shakespeare usually eliminates them before they can gain a hold. Dislocations of plot become clues to deeper unities, long and tedious speeches are seen as brilliant characterization. Shakespeare's authority lays on the reader the hermeneutical imperative: Read this play as important.
>
> (135)

It is certainly true that any exam question or essay assignment that asks "Discuss Shakespeare's use of metaphor" or "Investigate the way magic functions in the later plays" has the implicit final clause *and explain why this proves Shakespeare's greatness*. Many school students with a facility for getting high marks in English Lit classes realise that they are being marked partly on their skill at picking apart rhyme schemes and imagery, but also partly on their ability to relate these satisfactorily to the larger ideology of literary value. It is not enough to trace a pattern of metaphors through a poem; this must then be used as proof that the work is "effective", "emotional", "organic", or another term that implies a value judgement. A lot of students, teachers and readers find themselves instinctively making this move from describing features of the text to praising the work and its author. Even without explicit comments of this kind, it could be argued that the analysis itself bolsters the canonical position of the author, particularly when it happens within an educational setting that awards marks and qualifications for demonstrating the non-triviality of these texts. This often becomes visible only when it is done "badly"; when it is carried out in a way that fails to abide by the implied rules effectively enough, and thus highlights the switch between modes when an essay moves from analysis to ideology.

With Shakespeare the stakes are even higher: the process of literary discussion often seems set on proving Shakespeare not only great but greater than all others. Stephen Greenblatt's phrase "the conventional pieties of source study" sums this up well, pointing to the tendency to investigate the earlier texts Shakespeare drew upon only in the service of his status as a transcendent literary icon (94). "As a freestanding, self-sufficient, disinterested art work produced by a solitary genius, *King Lear* has only an accidental relationship to its sources," remarks Greenblatt ironically, "they provide a glimpse of the 'raw material' that the artist fashioned" (95). His comment underlines the way in which even rigorous and "factual" scholarship, such as the apparently dry issue of sources and textual influences, is often directed by assumptions about the relative value of the authors involved. The point about significance holds true in a broader sense: even in academia, where there are plenty of scholars who will argue Shakespeare's plots are banal, his ideas racist and his works potentially toxic, it is rare to find someone arguing that he is trivial and irrelevant.

According to Barton's second observation, Scripture is also assumed to have "contemporary relevance . . . to every generation, to all people at all times" (137). This is also a major feature of the way Shakespeare is discussed. Just as "Biblical characters were seen as typical of various human virtues or vices", many people are used to mentally categorising Othello as "jealousy" or Macbeth as "ambition" (137). Whether it is framed as "human nature" or "psychological accuracy", Shakespeare is believed to have produced narratives, figures and insights that will not cease to be relevant as social customs change. Shakespeare provides some sort of blueprint or deep code which remains the same through the centuries. Even when it is not spelled out in terms of timeless emotions, archetypes or wisdom, our society continually treats Shakespeare's works as a body of writing with "contemporary relevance". A good example is provided by the 2012 production of *Timon of Athens* at the National Theatre in London. The advertising material for this production called it a "strange fable of conspicuous consumption, debt and ruin", tying it to the recent economic crash, and featured a photograph of the actor playing Timon (Simon Russell Beale) at a party with figures clearly intended to be the footballer David Beckham, the former Prime Minister Tony Blair and the Mayor of London Boris Johnson. Reviews in the press accepted this claim to "relevance" as a central feature of their approval, declaring it "an urgent play for today", "a lacerating parable for our troubled times", "so relevant" and praising the director for "seizing the cynical disillusioned day. He hurls *Timon of Athens* into the 21st century and finds it lands there almost perfectly".[1]

However analogically "relevant" the sight of an Athenian nobleman sitting in the wilderness railing about sexually transmitted diseases might feel to reviewers in the middle of an economic crisis, there are plays from Shakespeare's period that are much more apt in a literal sense. *The Alchemist* and *A Chaste Maid in Cheapside* depict the commodifying of relationships and *The Witch of Edmonton* illustrates the way poor people are used as a scapegoat for a community's fears and economic insecurity. Indeed, the whole early modern genre known as "city comedy" spends its time attacking the money-obsessed, status-grubbing, debt-ridden world of London society. In other words, there are a handful of plays from the early seventeenth century which are literally about the city of which Boris Johnson is mayor, and where the National Theatre staged their production of *Timon*.

But the question of "relevance" in modern productions of drama from the sixteenth and seventeenth centuries is not simply a matter of matching up topics and themes. It is affected by prior assumptions about which playwrights are "relevant" or able to speak to our modern concerns (Shakespeare) and those who are of "historical" interest and can only speak about the period in which they lived (everyone else). The idea that the play has modern relevance is not solely based on recognising specific elements that have parallels in modern life, or that show unexpected continuities between the Elizabethan era and our own. It is based on a framework of interpretation that precedes the actual comparison of a play to modern life, one that has already positioned the work as a "sacred text" which will have something to say. As Barton points out, once a text has been designated as Scripture, readers are not continually subjecting it to tests in order to determine whether it qualifies. They are much more likely to read it in distinctively different ways from other books, without stopping after every paragraph to wonder whether they have read something in a non-sacred text that would fulfil the requirements just as well. Thus modern producers of Shakespeare do not trawl through the early modern theatre looking for works that might be "a lacerating parable

---

1. These reviews appeared on the National Theatre's own website, suggesting that they represented the kind of praise the theatre wanted associated with the show: the reviewers had understood and approved the production's intended meaning.

for our troubled times". They already assume that Shakespeare will fulfil that function, and performing *Timon* perpetuates that belief. It is not, after all, mainly a belief about the power of literature to reflect our lives today. That would be equally well served by staging the other plays I mentioned, and rather more specific insights might result. It is a belief that *Shakespeare* is always relevant, and will always be relevant. Putting on *Timon* after an economic crash caused by dubious lending practices amongst multinational finance corporations means that audiences and reviewers will be keenly watching for contemporary relevance even though the majority of them probably did not know the story, and perhaps had never heard of the play before. When that relevance was found, it fulfilled their expectations (and it is difficult to talk about this function of Shakespeare without straying into the language of prophecy) and is taken as "proof" of his universal relevance, strengthening the assumptions that led them to look for contemporary parallels in the first place.

"Relevance" also requires that the parallels produce an acceptable message, of course. Causing the audience to draw comparisons with the modern world is not enough, they must be drawn in a way that reflects positively on Shakespeare. For example, there is a play in the Shakespeare canon that arguably has a better claim than *Timon* to contemporary relevance in the aftermath of the 2008 economic crash. It involves the lending and re-lending of money, the commodification of people's bodies and romances in monetary terms, a parade of rich cosmopolitan characters from the multinational elite and the idea that one's self can be an investment project that will attract more capital. There is even an economic crash that leaves one character stranded when his debts are foreclosed. Thankfully, no major theatre (or any theatre that I am aware of) staged *The Merchant of Venice* in order to draw parallels with the unscrupulous lending in the sub-prime mortgage market, the implosion of over-leveraged merchant banks or the disaster of foreclosures for people who did not have the resources to adjust to the "credit crunch" as banks stopped lending. There was certainly plenty of extreme right-wing sentiment in the aftermath of the economic crisis, manifesting itself in anti-immigrant rhetoric in the popular press, conspiracy theories and street violence. However, the modern relevance that the audience at a cultural institution like the National Theatre expects to find in Shakespeare is not an Elizabethan concoction of racism, the scapegoating of minorities or anti-Semitic insinuations about the role of Jewish people in financial institutions. That kind of uncomfortable parallel is far more likely to be explained away as the result of Shakespeare's own time, rather than as part of his true message. Once again, the interpretation of Shakespeare, and what he has to say to us, is determined much more by the prior assumptions held about the "Scriptural" nature of his texts than by continually holding them up against those assumptions. Shakespeare is always relevant, but he is relevant in a way that fits our veneration of him.

The third aspect of treating texts as "Scripture" that John Barton identifies is an assumption of consistency. This is less striking for Shakespeare, since his plays are rarely used to produce explicit guidance or rules for life, unlike the Bible. Inconsistencies are less of an immediate problem if a reviewer does not feel it appropriate to cite lines from another Shakespeare play in order to prove that a certain production is inauthentic or missed Shakespeare's meaning. We do not tend to see controversies over Shakespeare in the same way that Christians debate the issue of female leadership in church or same-sex marriage, citing particular passages that support their view and call into question the other side's position. Nonetheless, the idea that Shakespeare is basically consistent underpins the way in which his plays are staged. The groundbreaking 1963/4 season of the Histories at the Royal Shakespeare Company has inspired a number of similar projects such as *Rose Rage* (an adaptation of the Henry VI plays into a sequential pair) and the BBC's history play sequence for the Cultural Olympiad which ran alongside the London Olympics in 2012. The subject matter, the plays' progress through vital moments of English history, and the fact that some characters reappear in different plays, make this an apparently obvious way to arrange performances. The panoramic vistas of English history, coupled with the struggles as a ruling house emerges, have captivated the audiences of these sequences.

This seems an obviously logical way to perform the history plays, at least it seems so once the Shakespeare canon is closed, printed and identified as a secular "Scripture". However, this involves imposing an order on the plays that is contradicted by our knowledge of Shakespeare's career. The first play to be written was the second *Henry VI*, followed by the third *Henry VI* which continues the story, and then the first *Henry VI*, which loops back in time to relate the events which preceded the other two. *Richard III*, which deals with the narrative after *3 Henry VI*, was the fourth to appear, after which Shakespeare jumped even further back to

produce a chronological run of four plays about events that pre-
dated all of the previous histories: *Richard II*, the two *Henry IVs*
and *Henry V*. If the historical events of the Histories run 1-2-3-4-
5-6-7-8, the composition order runs 6-7-5-8-1-2-3-4. The contents
page of the First Folio arranges the plays in order of their events,
imposing a consistency on their somewhat haphazard composition.
This involves crossing genre boundaries: *The Tragedie of King
Richard the third. Containing His treacherous Plots against his brother
Clarence: the pittiefull murther of his innocent nephews: his tyrannicall
usurpation: with the whole course of his detested life, and most deserved
death* becomes the "History" play we recognise as *Richard III*. The
tragic arc of rise, triumph and downfall, which finds parallels in
Macbeth or Marlowe's tyrant epic *Tamburlaine*, is plugged into the
canon of the Histories. That canon is interpreted via the tighter
dramaturgy and historical vision of the second tetralogy (*Richard
II, the two Henry IVs and Henry V*), whilst the diffuser and more
picaresque *Henry VI* plays are shuffled within the sequence and
brought under the scheme established by the later works. Given
this interpretative labour, it comes as no surprise that staging
"the Histories" usually involves a considerable quantity of cuts,
adjustment and general adaptation of the text. During preparations
for the 1963/4 season, for example, the RSC found they needed
to write a certain amount of cod-Shakespearean dialogue to paper
over the cracks. Shakespeare's vision of history is smoothed into a
coherent unity, demonstrating Barton's principle of "consistency"
against the evidence both of the texts and the historical facts.

The final principle is the idea that the Scriptural text contains an
excess of meaning, a "vision of the text as full of mysteries, with many
layers of meaning below the surface sense" (142). It is not exhausted
by a literal reading which spells out what the words apparently refer
to in a simple sense, but has the potential to release a host of hidden
meanings if it is studied for long enough. This approach ranges from
the idea that there are allegorical and symbolic meanings within the
Bible – which almost no-one would argue against – to methods
of reading that seek hidden codes and connections. The examples
Barton gives include the exegesis of Genesis 3:16 by Paul, in which
he argues that the fact that God made promises to Abraham "and
his seed" in the collective singular instead of using the plural means
that a single individual is meant, and that Jesus is that individual.
The grammatical detail, which does not affect the meaning of the
original line ("seed" is not an unusual form of words in Hebrew), is

read as if it carried a secret meaning that is only visible in retrospect. This secret meaning is almost parasitic on the first, existing as a code within the structure of the language. Likewise, Barton points out the practice of the Masoretes, a group of medieval Jewish scholars who demonstrated an enormous concern with the exact graphical form of the Scriptures – the precise letters and symbols used to write it – along with what sometimes appears to be indifference towards the meaning. "Meaning does not lie at the heart of the Masoretic text: what matters is the precise set of graphical forms given to Israel by God" (132).

Again, this may seem very far from any way that Shakespeare has been treated. However, there are examples of people seeking a coded meaning in the precise form of the plays, rather than their characters or meanings. James Shapiro has related the ingenious readings conspiracy theorists in the nineteenth century came up with to argue that "Shakespeare" was actually the pseudonym of Francis Bacon. In one version of this theory, Bacon had written the plays as a way of expressing his political discontent, and that of a small group of plotters around him. In order to reward those who were keen enough to sniff out his meaning, Bacon had allegedly encoded secret messages in the plays identifying himself and explaining his reasons. To reveal these messages, conspiracists treated Shakespeare's works like the Christian numerologists of Bacon's own time treated the Bible: assigning numbers to letters and words, seeking mathematical patterns that would point to the "true" meaning of the lines. Some sought the truth more laterally, and cut the collected works into long strips of paper to be wound round movable metal wheels, thinking that coherent sentences would emerge if the letters were read across the grain, if only the right combination of the wheels could be managed. Their failure was sometimes blamed on the way printers or editors had typeset the works: just like the Masoretes, these conspiracy theorists believed that the "true" meaning of Shakespeare was to be sought in the precise sequence of letters and punctuation marks, not in what those individual graphical characters meant when they were combined into words. This attitude even brings Shakespeare and the Bible together, in the urban legend that Psalm 46 in the King James Version was translated by Shakespeare. People have deduced this because you can find his name "hidden" in the text by counting forty-six words from the beginning and forty-six from the end, which correlate to the age he would have been when the KJV was translated. The story makes no attempt to explain how on earth the translators appointed by King James knew Shakespeare, or why a member of the entertainment industry which was viewed with suspicion by many clergy would have been asked to contribute to a religious project. This is not a historical theory at all, but a near-magical way of reading the text, which assumes that there are obscure codes hidden in it, running against the grain of its apparent meaning.

The concept of Scripture as a text with an excess of meaning is echoed and expanded in Rowan Williams' definition of a sacred text: "one for which the context is more than the social-ideological matrix" (224). He explains that approaching it involves

> a reading context that assumes a continuity between the world
> of the text and the world of the reader, and also assumes that
> reader and text are responding to a gift, an address or summons
> not derived from the totality of the empirical environment.
>
> (224)

In other words, a sacred text is one that points beyond itself and the situations in which it is written and read. We can explain and investigate the conditions that gave rise to it, and account for individual writers or the churches where it was produced, but the effect of the work as a whole is to call on the reader from outside their situation. The sacred text, in this view, speaks from elsewhere, disrupting the closed relationship between writer, reader and text. For Williams, we read Scripture "alert for 'deeper meanings'" because there is always more meaning to be unfolded (227). Just as there is more to a sacred text than the context of the writer, there is more to it than the situation of the reader: "the hearing of God at any one point does not exhaust God's speaking" and the text is "unresolved, unfinished, self-reflexive", pointing towards things it cannot contain (227).

We might expect this to be a claim specific to Biblical scholars, but similar statements can be found in comments on Shakespeare. Allan Bloom has stated that "Men may live more truly and fully in reading Plato and Shakespeare than at any other time, because then they are participating in essential being and forgetting their accidental lives" (380). The distinction between "accidental" parts of life, which are specific to time and circumstances, and the "essential being" which can be accessed by reading Shakespeare and Plato lifts the works out of historical contingency and places them amongst the eternal forms, allying these writers with the original source of reality that our world can only dimly reflect. The regular statements heard in newspapers and press releases about Shakespeare's "universality" slip past easily, but are making equally strong, apparently metaphysical, claims about him. Indeed, it is unclear whether "him" is the right pronoun for the Shakespeare that such statements imagine. They clearly cannot be referring to the historical person William Shakespeare who is designated by the will, property deeds and other legal documents that remain from the seventeenth century. Nor can "Shakespeare" in this sense mean a book of plays. Such assertions are about what the plays – whether read or performed – give us access to. Whether we call that creative imagination, a shared human nature, a transcendent genius, or simply a fiction (in either sense), they also invoke the "excess" beyond the social-historical-ideological context of reading and writing. Thus, both the way Shakespeare is treated and the way it is described seem to frame it as a sacred text or Scripture.

Reading (and Reading Reading)

In my discussion of Shakespeare and the Bible so far I have hurried over the word that precedes them in the title: *reading*. This word is central to the approach that *Words of Power* will take. In everyday life we use it in a variety of forms, as a noun and verb, with various shades of meaning in different contexts. Someone may announce from the lectern during a church service "A reading from the prophet Isaiah . . .", or an actor might explain "I'm reading for the part of Macbeth". An academic might praise "a particularly striking reading of *Henry V*" in a recent book – or might refer their class to "this week's reading". The activity of reading is often imagined as private and silent, but can equally be public and declarative. "Reading" can mean a set text, an interpretation of that text, an activity, a demonstration of skill or a legal intervention. The uses I have mentioned stress the ways in which reading can involve unlocking the meanings in a written text, but can also involve interpreting them, or even constructing meaning in dialogue with what is written. As we will see in later chapters, the process of reading also helps to construct the canon, to identify certain books as authoritative and to weave coherence between apparently disparate texts. When we come to an obscure or difficult passage, we are forced to confront our own activity as readers in making sense from what has been written. Unless we are willing to throw up our hands and assign the text no meaning whatsoever, we have to decide what a disputed or confusing line might mean. This is simply a more noticeable example of our continual involvement in the making of meaning, which takes place on a collective as well as an individual level. Reading is an active matter, and one of the concerns of this book is to trace how both Shakespeare and the Bible are read into the forms with which we are familiar.

In *Words of Power*, I will explore the history and use of the Bible and Shakespeare via this idea of reading the text into shape. The first two chapters are concerned with the canon and text: which books are included in the authoritative collections of the Bible and the works of Shakespeare, and which precise words are contained within those books. These might sound like issues that precede reading. After all, it is necessary to determine which plays are in the works of Shakespeare, and which words are in those plays, before beginning to read them. However, as I will show, both questions are tied up with how we read the books. Canonical and textual scholarship both involve intense reading of manuscripts: comparing, speculating, trying to make sense of the sources we possess. Textual criticism even uses the term "a reading" to refer to a particular variant of a text. These disciplines do not suspend the question of meaning until they have established in neutral and scientific terms which books are authentic and which versions of those books are to be accepted. They make decisions partly based upon the different meanings which those decisions would produce when the texts are read, and they test their theories against the resulting readings. Reading is an integral part of the search for the right list of books and the correct wording of their contents.

The third chapter looks at the different methods of interpretation that are applied to both collections, from spiritual allegory to feminist theory, and from character analysis to performance criticism. The huge variety of ways of reading these books highlights both the richness and depth that people have found in them, and the way meaning emerges as a co-operation between text and reader. Whilst it is not true that readers can find absolutely anything they want in Shakespeare or the Bible, using the reading tools of Marxist theory will produce a drastically different interpretation from the one arrived at with the reading tools of rhetorical criticism.

The fourth chapter looks at reading in a more practical sense, concentrating on the differences between public performance and private silent reading. As with theories of interpretation, the way the texts are performed can shape the sorts of meanings which emerge. Public and private performance suppose different intentions on the part of those engaging with the books, and history is full of writers who harboured suspicions about those who performed them in the "wrong" ways. Some extreme examples are included, in order to tease out why people thought the way they did, notably Charles Lamb's insistence in the nineteenth century that Shakespeare cannot really be performed on stage without ruining it, and St. Augustine's passive-aggressive justification of St. Ambrose reading the Bible to himself, despite how suspicious such an activity might appear.

The fifth and sixth chapters expand the scope of "reading" to consider some examples of the ways in which Shakespeare and the Bible are used in non-theatrical and non-religious contexts. Adverts, state ceremonies and novels are only a few of the contexts in which the words of these books appear. These all constitute "readings" in that they impose a certain interpretation on the words. A judge, a general or a politician quoting Shakespeare is doing so because they believe the words have a particular meaning, and one that serves their purpose. A poet who embeds Biblical echoes in their writing does so to pick up certain resonances and draw out certain implications. Both these examples involve assigning a meaning to the words, thus reflecting back upon the original text. They are interpretations that can add another layer of meaning to the work from which they come. How much of our understanding of both books is built up from hearing them quoted and adapted in other contexts? Shakespeare's works and the Bible both hold associations in our public culture that sometimes have very little to do with the actual words contained within them.

As those summaries might suggest, a considerable part of this book's exploration of the reading of Shakespeare and the Bible will involve looking at the past. This is not entirely because we cannot understand our current ways of reading without first learning about hundreds of years of history – although that can give us a firmer grasp of what we do and why we do it – but because history can provide useful surprises. These two texts are such an established part of our cultural landscape that it is easy to take them for granted, and assume that the ways we treat them are natural and inevitable. Noticing a monk who mused on the four different meanings enclosed in one word, or a seventeenth-century playwright who rewrote *King Lear* to give it a happy ending, can bring us up with a salutary shock. It forces us to deal with the fact that our own attitudes to these sacred texts are particular and time-bound. They are the result of historical and social conditions which we cannot always see, but which have a deep influence on us. The Russian literary critic Viktor Shlovsky described the potential for "defamiliarisation" in literature, meaning its capacity to show us the world in arresting and startling ways.[1] For him it was part of art's function to stop us taking the world around us for granted, to make it strange and striking by forcing us to break our automatic habits of perception and confront the weirdness that surrounded us. History can function in a similar way, jolting us out of our ruts and bringing us face to face with people who also thought theirs was the only natural way to do things. Part of the purpose of *Words of Power* is to help us look again at our own religious and literary reading, and to see it as bizarre, outrageous, eccentric and obscure.

With that in mind, it is inevitable that my own historical and social situation will affect the way I have written this work. As a British academic specialising in literature, and a member of the Church of England, my approach to these texts will be deeply informed by my education, the institutions I have worked within, and all my experiences of Shakespeare and the Bible, from convivial weekends in Stratford-upon-Avon to taking part in the Liturgy of the Word in an eight-hundred-year-old parish church. The examples I have selected, and the way in which I have discussed them, will be tinged by my own outlook and the influences that have shaped me.[2] Nonetheless, I hope that I have drawn widely enough that most readers in Britain and the US will recognise the general outlines of the literary and religious cultures I have sketched, and find something valuable in examining their history and diversity, even if their own specific situation is rather different in detail. In fact, those readers whose experiences differ might find it easiest to see the oddness and particularity of the modern reading worlds I mention.

---

1. A good account of the term is given in Makaryk, p. 528.
2. Whilst consulting a certain edition of the works of Irenaeus of Lyons, the second-century bishop and theologian, I was amused to find a note from the editor describing the way in which Irenaeus appeals to all parts of the Christian church, and is thus claimed as a forerunner by Roman Catholics, Lutherans, Baptists, Methodists and so on. This was particularly amusing to me, as the briefest perusal of Irenaeus' theological writings will show clearly that he was an Anglican, probably educated at an independent school in the south of England, and most likely with an appreciation of cricket, bitter ale and the novels of Dorothy L. Sayers.

1.
The Text Itself (I):
Questions about the Canon

Before reading Shakespeare and the Bible, it is worth giving some
thought to what collection of works we mean by those names.
Given the layout of most modern editions, in order to get to the
text a reader usually has to turn over a contents page which lists
the individual parts of the book and where we can find them. It is
one of the first pieces of information with which they are presented,
and can help to organise the experience of reading. However, those
modern editions are the result of centuries of history, during some
of which the Bible and the works of Shakespeare did not exist in
the form that we know. The "canon" is a term used in both Biblical
and literary studies, usually referring to an authoritative collection
of books. It has been the subject of controversy in both fields over
recent decades, as ideas of authority are questioned, contested and
subjected to historical scrutiny. In this chapter I will consider where
the official collections of Shakespeare and the Bible emerged from,
the factors which influenced their development, and some of the
books that did not make it into the authoritative lists.

The Books of the Bible (and Whose Bible)

Both those who hold traditional views about the canon of the
Christian Bible, and those who are more sceptical, tend to stress that
the final shape of the canon was not the result of a single meeting or a
single person's opinion. F.F. Bruce, for example, who ascribes a high
level of reliability to the documents as we possess them, declares:

> One thing must be emphatically stated. The New Testament
> books did not become authoritative for the Church because
> they were formally included in an authoritative list; on the
> contrary, the Church included them in her canon because

she already regarded them as divinely inspired, recognizing
their innate worth and generally apostolic authority, direct
or indirect . . . what these councils did was not to impose
something new upon the Christian communities but to codify
what was already the general practice of those communities.

(27)

For Bruce the process was one of "recognition", in which the
councils officially stated what church communities already knew: that
these documents were inspired and contained the word of God. He
suggests in the same chapter that any modern reader can demonstrate
for themselves how correct the councils were by reading any of the
"apocryphal" Gospels that were not included in the final canon. This
suggests that the canonical process is relatively unproblematic and
uncontentious, since the real activity has already taken place in the
inspiration of the documents. (Which is not to say that Bruce did
not take the insights of Biblical criticism very seriously, as a scholar.)

The more sceptical attitude typified by the work of Bart Ehrman
also sees the canonisation process as dependent upon the existing
practices of Christian communities. Ehrman remarks that the "New
Testament did not drop from a sky a few weeks after Jesus died or
after Paul finished writing his books", and emphasises the role of
conflict and power in the formation of the canon, against Bruce's
process of "recognition" (381).

The movement to define a canon was thus, in large part, a
product of the conflicts between what we have been calling
orthodoxy and heresy. These conflicts were waged in order to
win converts to one point of view or another. The side that
won these conflicts was the side that decided what Christian
belief would be for all time to come . . . [and] claimed they
had always been the majority view within the religion. And
they appealed to their own books to prove it, and rejected
the books of the other groups. And so Matthew, Mark, Luke,
and John were "in", and the Gospels of Peter, Thomas, James
and Mary were "out". It was all a matter of having written
authorities to support your views.

(378-9)

This reading of early Christian history sees the shape of the
canon as the outline of conflicts between different versions of the
faith, a retrospectively assembled collection of books that tell the

most convenient story for the winners in an ideological conflict. It obviously differs very significantly from Bruce's description of a church which received the Scriptures from the Apostles and those who followed them, venerated the books for their transparent holiness, and used them in religious life until the official decisions simply rubber-stamped what everyone knew to be the correct contents page of the Bible. Nonetheless, both scholars – with their drastically varying accounts of how the Bible came to contain the texts it does – are careful to describe its origin in terms of Christian communities and their religious lives. The shape of the Bible as we have it (in its various versions) emerged from the devotional and theological activities of Christian groups; its use for these purposes preceded its definitive borders or officially-stated limits. In other words, the Bible was being read long before there was any agreement over what exactly the Bible contained. Furthermore, those ways of reading the texts that became the Bible produced an understanding of the Christian faith that in turn informed the decisions as to what should be included in its Scriptures. The Bible was, in this sense, read into existence.

The emergence of the Christian canon is a complex story stretching from the early second century to the fifth, and a number of criteria were used to determine which books counted as authoritative when the canon came to be closed. As Lee Martin McDonald points out, these criteria varied between the early churches, and when the same principles were used by different groups, they were frequently given different weight. However, the following list covers the major criteria used by the early church to justify the inclusion of particular books in the canon. In some ways this list complements John Barton's list of ways people treat Scripture which I cited in the introduction; they both overlap and diverge. The reasons people provide for considering a work to be divinely inspired do not always match up with the way they treat that book in practice. It is also important to remember that these criteria do not precede Barton's list: there was not a stage during which a selection of books were officially canonised, followed by an era in which people treated them as Scriptural. It was only because they were already held in high esteem that they made it into the closed canon, and that closed canon then had its own impacts on the treatment of these books. The canonical process is the history of institutions trying to get to grips with which religious writings (already in use) should be considered normative for their understanding of God, and of themselves.

A major qualifying feature for books in the New Testament is apostolic authorship. There were disagreements (as there still are) over the ascription of particular books to particular apostles, but there was a general agreement that "the apostolic witness" was a vital way of "ensuring that the church's tradition was not severed from its historical roots and proximity to Jesus, the primary author of the early church" (McDonald, 407). When discussing the Gospels, the early church father Tertullian distinguishes between "apostles" and "apostolic men" – between those who were named companions of Jesus such as Matthew and John, and those who were members of their movement such as Luke – and gives greater authority to the writings of the former. Of course, there is no simple correlation between books that were identified as having been written by apostles, and the eventual canon. A number of gospels with the names of apostles attached were ruled out of the final collection, such as that of St. Thomas, and the practice of pseudoepigraphy (writing new works under the name of a famous person) meant that not every book in the New Testament is there on the basis of apostolic authorship. Indeed, McDonald argues that the validation of the Letter to the Hebrews as written by St. Paul (after considerable controversy amongst the early church) "may have stemmed from the desire to get a cherished writing into the canon rather than from the sincere belief that Paul actually wrote it" (408). Apostolic authorship may in some cases have been the official sign of acceptance for a work that was already venerated and used for other reasons.

The doctrinal content of the writings bequeathed to the churches by previous generations was also the basis for decisions about canonical status. The bishop Serapion argued against using the Gospel of Peter on the basis of this criterion, judging that it did not conform to correct beliefs about Jesus. "[The book's] theology was considered out of step with the 'rule of faith' operating in the church", despite it fulfilling other criteria such as being ascribed to a major apostle and possessing considerable antiquity (McDonald, 410). Given the variety of theologies and understandings of the Christian message during the early centuries, the criterion of orthodoxy does not mean that the books eventually settled upon present a unified and single vision of the faith. These books were part of varying Christian practices, and after canonisation they continued to give rise to a range of new understandings, many of which conflicted with each other. However, there are basic elements that appear in common, such as belief in one God, and in Jesus as redeemer, along with theological themes like divine wisdom, miracles and the nature of faith.

The use of books by the existing church communities operated as a criterion in several ways. It supplied a basic set of materials from which the canonical works could emerge; after all, these criteria were not applied to any passing book of religious teaching, but only those which were already part of the churches' life. It provided a test of catholicity (or universality), as both beliefs and texts could be compared between local churches to identify those held in common, and those which were regarded as most central to the faith (not always the same thing). It also provided a rough test of how a work could contribute to the life of faith, what spiritual "fruits" might manifest themselves in the community that employed a work in their worship and teaching. Thus the fact that a text had been used and revered by a church for some years was a logical influence on its inclusion in the canon, since it had already been fulfilling the functions needed from a Scriptural work. A book that had enabled believers to carry out their religious practices, and that had enriched their communal life as Christians, could justifiably be considered for canonical status. The debates (and eventual agreements) over which books were included in the Bible were also debates over which local churches should be regarded as part of an orthodox Christian tradition, and which should be excluded as heretical. "The struggle about the New Testament canon . . . was between different factions within the church about the true interpretation of the tradition and the true identity of the church", since "the canon is the foundation of the collective identity of the church" (Borsten, 193 in Thomassen). It would be a mistake to suggest that the criterion of use was nakedly "political" and cynical, since that would rather assume that all Christians were standing at year zero of the church with the same documents available to everyone, trying to discern which were closest to the word of God. In fact, the closing of the canon involved a number of churches, which had all developed their own (albeit overlapping) collections of texts, trying to recognise the essential elements of the Christian tradition in their various forms of devotion. Being influenced by another church's view of the canon was part of accepting them as fellow Christians and affirming their vision of the faith.

Canons and Kinds of Canon

Having examined some of the causes and criteria that led to books being included in the Biblical collection and regarded as canonical, we can also note the multiple meanings that are contained in the idea of "canonical" books. So far I have been using the term to mean part of the officially-recognised collection of authoritative texts, but it is possible to distinguish at least two forms of canonical status: "open" and "closed" canonicity. Though they are both implied by the modern use of the term "canon" (and the uses that are made of canonical books), they were not necessarily synonymous throughout the history of the Bible.

"Open" canonicity is the situation where a particular set of writings or oral traditions are recognised by a religious group as having authoritative status. They possess a special position in the group's regard as inspired, powerful, normative or divine. "Closed" canonicity applies to writings or traditions that are identified as the *only* inspired or normative works for a religious group, when a "fixed list of authoritative Scriptures" has been established (McDonald, 57). This distinction helps to explain the apparent conflicts between some pieces of evidence from the early church about how the Bible was regarded, and contributes to a clearer understanding of the historical process from which it emerged. There were books that had the force of "open" canon during the first centuries of Christianity, but that did not make the cut for the "closed" canon.

It also has implications beyond the elucidation of that particular story, providing us with a more nuanced sense of canonicity and separating the concepts of authority and limitation which are often bound up together. For example, the admonishment in Deuteronomy 4:2 to "neither add anything to what I command you nor take anything from it, but keep the commandment of the Lord your God with which I am charging you" implies both authority and limitation. All these writings are inspired, and only these. The same principles can be seen in Revelation 22:18-9's warning that "if anyone adds to [these words], God will add to that person the plagues described in this book; if anyone takes away from the words of the book of this prophecy, God will take away that person's share in the tree of life and in the holy city". The even more famous statement in 2 Timothy 3:16 that "All Scripture is inspired by God and is useful for teaching, for reproof, for correction, and for training in righteousness" only explicitly advances an open canonicity. In order to argue for a closed sense in this verse, it would be necessary to provide evidence that "Scripture" was understood at the time as a closed and limited collection of writings, so that the line would be understood as "the group of writings we all know to be the only repository of God's word is useful for . . ."

There is also a possible alternative translation of the first words as "Every scripture [which is] inspired by God is also useful for . . ." which would make the line a piece of advice on how to employ the writings already generally agreed to be inspired. Indeed, the idea that these verses are statements about the Bible, rather than their own particular books, rests on an assumption that the canonising process has already taken place. The citation of 2 Timothy by fundamentalists, and those who hold to a doctrine of Biblical inerrancy, presumes that it is obvious to everyone what "Scriptures" are, and that a definitive list exists somewhere. Likewise, the verses from Deuteronomy and Revelation are only explicitly warnings about the particular section of text they appear in, and only count as a statement about the Bible if that Bible has already been recognised as a cohesive whole, and the two books accepted as part of it. Thus even apparently clear and straightforward statements about the authority of the Bible frequently depend on intertwined assumptions about the various meanings of "canon".

Open and closed canonicity can also be seen in particular episodes that influenced the form the canon eventually took. Halfway through the second century there appeared a version of Christianity known as Marcionism, named after the Roman shipping magnate who founded it.[1] Marcion's ideas involved the rejection of the God of the Old Testament as an inferior and even evil being, who was contrasted with the just and wise Supreme God revealed in Christianity. He believed that Jesus was sent by the true God to replace the Law, and thus to do away with the Jewish Scriptures. Marcion regarded the Gospels – and the majority of the Apostles – as having misunderstood Jesus' significance and message. In his view, Paul's writings provided a truer account of the meaning of Christianity, and even they were subject to "Judaizing" influences. He constructed a radically smaller canon, rejecting the entire Old Testament and accepting only the Pauline epistles and Luke's Gospel. He also edited his selected books rigorously, to bring them into line with his theology and root

---

1. A description of Marcion and his context is provided in MacCulloch's *A History of Christianity*, pp. 125-8; he also discusses Montanism from p. 138 onwards.

out what he considered to be interpolations of incorrect doctrine. Marcion's movement influenced the orthodox canon of Christianity, not by changing the array of books regarded as authoritative, but by forcing other early Christian writers to insist on the validity of the works he discarded. His effect was to foreground the open element of canonicity – the belief in a range of inspired writings – demonstrated by the Church Fathers' refusal to accept such a reduced collection of Scriptures.

The opposite impact was produced by the Montanists, also known as the New Prophecy, an apocalyptic group who appeared in Asia Minor during the latter part of the second century. Though claiming continuity with Christianity (like Marcion), they also claimed that their priests and priestesses, Montanus, Priscilla and Maximilla, were receiving a series of oracles from the Holy Spirit. They gathered their movement at a town called Pepouza, where they believed the apocalypse would soon take place, and held ecstatic religious services. The oracles they produced were collected as a new group of revelations from God, to be revered alongside the Old Testament and the various apostolic writings about Jesus. When the bishops of the churches around Asia Minor came to declare Montanism a heresy, the group's production of "new" Scriptures had an effect on attitudes to the canon of other inspired writings. Just as Marcion's reduced collection caused an insistence on the validity of the books regarded as inspired, the Montanists' outpouring of prophecy produced a reaction that speeded up the closing of the canon. It also caused suspicion to be cast on apocalyptic writings in general, such as Revelation. Neither Marcionism nor Montanism were the main influences on the formation of a New Testament canon: there were already collections of inspired writings circulating, and a notion of canonicity was already developed. However, they did exert an impact from opposite directions, and we can see the notions of open and closed canonicity being asserted in the wider church's reaction to the two movements.

Practical Canons and Canonical Practices

From this brief exploration, it will be obvious that dating the origin of the New Testament canon is far from simple. It is not possible to specify precisely when the collection of writings we know as the canon came together and were generally recognised. We can, however, look at the stages through which the New Testament passed on its way to a modern sense of the canon, and the evidence we possess for when these took place. The use to which early Christian writers put the books which later became the Bible gives us a sense of how they viewed them. For example, Justin Martyr, writing in the second century, refers to the Gospels as the "memoirs of the Apostles" and relates that they and the Old Testament prophets were read in meetings of Christians on Sundays (in Richardson, 287). His reference to both the Gospels and the Old Testament elsewhere shows that he considered them as authoritative when deciding points of doctrine. He does not, however, mention Paul's letters. We can only draw limited conclusions from this: it is difficult to argue from absence and suggest that Paul was not authoritative for Justin, but we can note that he leaned more heavily in his works on the Gospels and the prophets. We also cannot assume that Justin had a fixed canon in mind, from which he selected individual works when he needed a Scriptural authority. If he had any such closed canon, there is no evidence of it in his works: we can only conclude that he regarded the Gospels and prophets as inspired in the "open" sense of canonicity mentioned above.

The bishop and theologian Irenaeus marks a shift in the treatment of the New Testament documents in the late second century, as he consistently refers to them as "Scriptures". This accords them a significant level of authority, and also puts them in the same category as the Scriptural books that Christianity inherited from Judaism. When the Gospels record Jesus expounding the Scriptures at Capernaum, or quoting them in his controversies with the Pharisees, it is obviously the older collection that is meant. However, from the time of Irenaeus onwards, it became common practice amongst Christians to refer to later documents as "Scriptures", even if they disagreed on which precise documents should be given that label (McDonald, 289-90). Irenaeus also put forward very definite views on which books he thought counted as Scripture, including this statement on the Gospels:

> It is not possible that the Gospels can be either more or fewer in number than they are. For, since there are four zones of the world in which we live, and four principal winds, while the Church is scattered throughout all the world and while the "pillar and ground" of the Church is the Gospel and the spirit of life, it is fitting that she should have four pillars, breathing out immortality on every side, and vivifying men afresh. From

this fact, it is evident that the Word, the Artificer of all, who sits upon the cherubim and who contains all things and was manifested to men, has given us the Gospel under four aspects, but bound together by one spirit. . . .

(in McDonald, 291)

As scholars including Lee Martin McDonald and John Barton have pointed out, this is a remarkable piece of argument, and does not seem to operate along normal lines of logic, even for the early church.[1] It would be a mistake to read this passage as if it proved that everyone in the late second century knew there were only four Gospels. The elaborate form in which Irenaeus' statement is cast, and the vigour with which he insists that there could only ever have been four Gospels, rather goes to prove that other opinions were entirely possible. If everyone had agreed to the four that later became canonical, he would not have needed to expend such energy on declaring any other opinion entirely beyond the pale, dragging in such odd logic to do so.

By the time of Athanasius, in the fourth century, another major shift occurred: he is "probably the first to use to term *canon* . . . in reference to a closed body of sacred literature" (McDonald, 380). In Athanasius' writing the Christian Scriptures are both inspired and limited to a certain collection of books, and he is the first to record a list that corresponds with the modern New Testament. Of course this does not mean that by Athanasius' time the matter was settled, nor that everyone recognised that he was right as soon as he circulated the list. Looking at history from the early twenty-first century, it is easy to fall into the assumption that it is inevitably leading towards us, and that the modern NT canon – like baked beans, democracy or the symphony – was somehow waiting to be discovered. The fact that Athanasius drew up a list of the same books does not mean that the New Testament sprang into existence that year and everyone recognised it as right. The process of canonical development continued, and other collections continued to be used

---

1. Though agreeing on this, they draw somewhat different conclusions from the unusual form of the argument. Barton argues in *How the Bible Came To Be* that the forced quality to the reasoning shows that the four Gospels were already a given fact for Irenaeus himself, and at least for the area in which he wrote (p. 45). McDonald takes the line I have followed here: that the odd argument shows Irenaeus was arguing energetically against other opinions which definitely did exist, and was forced to use whatever arguments he could fashion from analogies or instances of the number four (*Biblical Canon*, p. 291).

by other churches. Nonetheless, his writings do mark a noticeable point when we can first see a collection that corresponds to our modern one. Athanasius also displays an interesting attitude to some of the books excluded from his canon: he names books that are not canonical, but are worthy of reading and learning from.

> But for the sake of being more exact in detail, I also add this admonition, writing out of necessity, that there are also other books apart from these that are not indeed in the above list, but were produced by our ancestors to be read by those who are just coming forward to receive oral instruction in the word of true religion. These include the Wisdom of Solomon, the Wisdom of Sirach, Esther, Judith, Tobias, the so-called Teaching of the Apostles, and the Shepherd.
>
> (in McDonald, 380)

In adding this comment, Athanasius makes clear that there is still some variation in what counts as a canonical book, or some variation between more and less canonical works. The books he lists here include some which are in the modern Roman Catholic canon, such as Esther and Judith, as well as some that do not appear in any modern Bible, such as the Teaching of the Apostles and the Shepherd (usually known today as the Didache and the Shepherd of Hermas). Intriguingly, these near-canonical works are apparently to be used to instruct those who are new to Christian faith, giving the impression that they are somehow more accessible, whether because of their style or the later date of some of them. Perhaps Athanasius envisioned them in the way modern Christians might think of the works of Charles Spurgeon or Augustine of Hippo: later works that are authoritative and venerable, and effective in expounding religious truth, but not technically inspired. It is worth noting that the bishop advises that these semi-canonical books be available to new Christians, rather than insisting that they be trained only on fully-inspired works to ensure they did not pick up any dubious doctrines, and leaving the less canonical works to more mature believers who could sift the truth from them.

The Parallel Traditions (and the Newly "Old" Testament)

So far I have been discussing the canon of the Christian Bible as if only the New Testament were at stake. There are certainly some people who believe that by the time of Jesus the Jewish Scriptures were a stable and widely-recognised collection. In their account, Christianity inherited a complete and defined canon from Judaism, and set about constructing interpretations of those writings which made sense of the revelation they had received through the life and death of Christ.

However, others have questioned this view. McDonald highlights the fact that, just as with the NT, we can only construct an approximate sense of which books were considered canonical by citations and references in early Christian writings. These have to be handled with some care; as he points out, Paul quotes the Greek poet Aratus in the Book of Acts, and no-one has suggested that the Greek poets were included in the Christian canon (192). The same complexities about "open" and "closed" canonicity apply to the Scriptures that originated within Judaism.

We know that the early Christians generally used the Greek translation of the Jewish Scriptures, known as the Septuagint. This translation had been made by Jewish scholars in Alexandria, in response to the dispersion of Jewish people within the Greek-speaking world, and it also made the books available to those outside Jewish culture. There was thus already a version of the Jewish Scriptures available in the common language of the region where Christianity appeared, and in which the early Christian wrote their own documents. As part of the ongoing development of Judaism, some books were included in the Septuagint that had not been regarded as authoritative before (including the book of Maccabees) and others were included that had been composed in Greek without ever being part of the Hebrew collection (such as the second book of Maccabees and the Wisdom of Solomon).

As Christianity and Judaism diverged more and more sharply during the latter half of the first century and the Roman conquest of Jerusalem, the emerging Rabbinic movement within Judaism emphasised the Hebrew versions of the Scriptures over the Septuagint, which had come to be associated with Christians. As Rabbinic Judaism and Christianity developed in different directions, with one constructing the Talmud and the other the New Testament, they already had slightly different collections of sacred books. These collections defined the identity of the groups using them, just as the early Christian controversies over the canon were partly disagreements about the identity of the Church.

Continuing Controversy and Long Divisions

The issue of the canon did not entirely end when a stable collection emerged at the end of the fourth century. Anyone browsing the Bibles available in a bookshop today might notice that there are some contents that vary from Bible to Bible. Several of the books that were included in the Septuagint are the subject of controversy: for example, Evangelical Protestants accept only the twenty-four that survive in Hebrew versions, whereas the Greek Orthodox Church ascribes equal authority to the books that were composed in Greek (or only survive in Greek). The Roman Catholic Church accepts a smaller number of the extra books of the Septuagint, whilst the Anglican Church only regards the twenty-four Hebrew books as canonical, but advises in its Articles of Religion that the extra books can be read "for example of life and instruction of manners" (*BCP*, 613). These variations stem from the emphasis at the time of the Reformation on returning "to the source" of the Bible, and translating from the original Hebrew. The Reformers' focus on stripping away church tradition and the accretions of the centuries which stood between believers and the living voice of the Gospels led them to pare away the later books, and even to cast doubt on the authority of some New Testament books. Luther's German translation of the Bible, for example, printed Hebrews, James, Jude and Revelation after the other New Testament books, with a distinct space on the contents between this group and the rest, to mark them out. He also referred to James as "an epistle of straw" at one point, due to its stress on the necessity of good works rather than the all-sufficient faith in which Luther believed.

The distinctions between the contents of modern Bibles are probably not a major factor in the religious lives of most Christians today. There are some doctrinal differences that hinge on the excluded works: the Roman Catholic belief in the efficacy of prayers for the dead is often backed up by reference to the book of Maccabees, where such prayers are sanctioned by the narrative. However, the details of religious life are probably more informed by the wider Christian traditions and denominations where believers find themselves, than by the precise point at which the Septuagint was translated and what it contained. Indeed, the technical disagreements between the denominations over such matters show that they agree on much more serious canonical issues, such as the ideas that a canon is a fixed collection of works that has been closed for centuries, and the contents of which are verbally fixed and authoritative.

Shakespeare's Canon and Canons of Shakespeare

Understanding the Shakespearean canon requires some of the same kind of historical unpicking as the Biblical canon, though with a less imposing gap of time and slightly simpler principles. At first glance it might seem an extremely simple matter to determine the right books to include in Shakespeare's Complete Works: find the ones with his name on the title page and print them in the same volume. However, the conditions under which the books were printed, the situation in which Shakespeare wrote, and the concept of authorship that was around at the time all have a complicating effect.[1]

The idea of a "collected works" of Shakespeare was one that only appeared after Shakespeare himself was no longer around. Printed editions of his plays had been in circulation during Shakespeare's life, in the cheap one-volume format called "quartos" that had a similar place to modern paperbacks. However, it was not until after his death that a collection was made and published in 1623 with his name as the defining feature. The project was undertaken by John Heminges and Henry Condell, actors who had worked with Shakespeare, and was one of the first collections of plays from the public theatre industry to appear as the "collected works" of a writer. The previous example, Ben Jonson's volume of his own *Works* in 1616, had attracted derision and mockery for daring to consider stage plays as artistic work worthy of appearing in such a collection. From our vantage point in the twenty-first century, at the end of a few hundred years during which Shakespeare has been considered the greatest writer in English, if not in history, the idea of a collected works seems not only natural but necessary. This tends to obscure a couple of factors about the First Folio that make it different from the works of subsequent writers, and which might alter the way we think about the book.

The First Folio was posthumous: Shakespeare died in 1616, and the collection of his works did not appear until 1623. They were explicitly dedicated to continuing his memory, and framed

---

1. My account of Shakespeare's canon, transmission and text in these two chapters draws particularly on John Jowett's *Shakespeare and Text* and Andrew Murphy's *A Concise Companion to Shakespeare and the Text*, both of which cover these issues in erudite and accessible ways.

as a monument to his talent. This is not necessarily very different from modern writers; for obvious reasons, the complete works of a number of later authors have only appeared once the prospect of any further writings had been settled in the most final way. However, there is a greater disconnection in the First Folio between author and final edition than we are accustomed to, since it was a collection of works that had not been written for print publication. The plays had appeared in print before his death, but only in the cheap and perishable editions known as "quartos" and "octavos". These flimsy and inexpensively printed copies were often more associated with the theatre company that had staged the show than with the author who had written the script. The first printed edition of *Romeo and Juliet* declared on its title page: "*An Excellent conceited Tragedie of Romeo and Juliet. As it hath been often (with great applause) plaid publiquely by the Right Honourable the L[ord] Hunsdon his Servants. London. Printed by John Danter, 1597.*" The book tries to persuade the passing shopper to purchase it by referring to its qualities ("excellent", "conceited"), by the acclamation it has received in the theatre ("with great applause") and the company who performed it ("L[ord] Hunsdon his Servants"). Nowhere does it suggest that anyone might want to read it because William Shakespeare had written it. Later quartos used the playwright's name, but they remained associated with the theatre much more than a Romantic notion of a solitary genius producing self-sufficient works of art.

Thus when Shakespeare's name does appear on a play printed in quarto format, we should ask ourselves what function it performs. There were no copyright laws for authors in early modern London, so putting a writer's name on the book version of a play did not have the same sort of legal force as it would today. It was more likely to have been intended as a marketing ploy, to attract customers who had become familiar with Shakespeare's reputation either via his plays or his non-dramatic poetry. (The latter had been published under his name in the mid-1590s.) By the turn of the century, ten years into Shakespeare's writing career for the stage, quarto editions of his plays began to appear with his name on them: the second printing of *Richard III* and *Love's Labour's Lost* in 1598; *Romeo and Juliet* in 1599; *2 Henry IV*, *Much Ado About Nothing*, *A Midsummer Night's Dream* and *The Merchant of Venice* in 1600. These were all published with the declaration that they were written by "William Shakespeare" or "W. Shakespeare". Others of his plays continued to be printed without an authorial attribution, such as *Henry V*, but this marks the point at which it was apparently worth putting Shakespeare's name on his plays to attract customers. The value of this name seems to be confirmed by the fact that in 1605, a play called *The London Prodigal* was printed with Shakespeare's name attached, and 1608 saw *A Yorkshire Tragedy* appear with a similar claim. Modern scholarship does not believe that either can be safely or realistically ascribed to Shakespeare, nor can *Thomas Lord Cromwell* (1602) or *The Puritan* (1607) which both claimed their author to be "W.S." An ascription on the title page that claimed William Shakespeare as author (or winked in that direction) appears to have become a worthwhile addition to a play book by this decade.[1] However, quartos of his earlier works that had already been selling successfully did not all acquire his name on their title page; mere accuracy as to their authorship does not seem to have been a motive for adding it. So after about ten years of writing for the stage, Shakespeare's name became a useful marker of value in publishing play books, but this did not mean that all his plays were published with his name, nor that all the plays that went under his name had been written by him.

This brings us to a related point that distinguishes the First Folio from modern collected editions of a writer's work: the contents are theatrical, not literary, documents. The plays in the First Folio are not simply the pre-performance code waiting to be brought to life by the addition of actors and scenery: they have already been through the theatrical system, and have potentially been altered by it. They may have been intended for publication, and the author might have regarded them as literary works, but none of Shakespeare's plays, in the versions that we have, came straight from his pen as self-contained works of art in the versions that we possess. Any Shakespeare play in the *Collected Works* was written for a specific theatre company (often with particular parts tailored to the particular actors) and may have been adapted or changed during production, then passed through the various stages of printing. This may have altered the play to the extent of adding entirely new sequences: many scholars believe that the text of *Macbeth* included in the First Folio had been adapted by the playwright Thomas Middleton. Stage writers are known to have written extra material for plays in the repertory to keep them fresh: there were additions to the Elizabethan stalwart play *The Spanish Tragedy* (possibly written by Shakespeare, Ben Jonson or another

---

1. This argument is made at much more length by Lukas Erne in *Shakespeare and the Book Trade*.

contemporary) and it is entirely possible that Shakespeare's own plays were treated in the same way. After all, these were the scripts of a working theatre company that needed to keep the audience entertained in order to pay their bills. They were not sacrosanct literary works at this stage. So Middleton appears to have added material from his own play *The Witch* to Macbeth, including an appearance from the goddess Hecate and a couple of songs. We are also faced with the problem of two versions of *King Lear*, which differ from each other for a total of four hundred lines. As Emma Smith points out, the variations affect serious interpretative issues such as when Lear dies and whether he thinks Cordelia is still alive at the time (*Introduction*, 64). Whether Shakespeare was involved in changing the text, and whatever series of events produced these two different versions, we cannot simply regard the First Folio as containing *King Lear*. It includes a *King Lear*, which bears an unknown relationship to whatever Shakespeare might originally have written, or originally have intended.

In fact, there is one play document that we believe is an autograph, meaning it is Shakespeare's own words in Shakespeare's own handwriting. *Sir Thomas More* is not the most famous of the works attributed to him, but it may be the only theatrical manuscript that includes Shakespeare writing out his own lines. Three pages, including a speech in which the eponymous lawyer appeals to a rioting crowd who object to immigrants in London, are written in handwriting designated "Hand D" by scholars, and believed by many to be Shakespeare's. This might sound like the perfect Shakespearean document, the one in which there can be absolutely no doubt that what he wrote was what he meant. It is the ultimate authentic work, with no confusing layers between the author's hand and our eyes. On the contrary, *Sir Thomas More* plunges us even further into the ambiguities of early modern stage writers. The play was written by Henry Chettle and Anthony Munday, but then rewritten later by a group including Thomas Dekker, Thomas Heywood and Shakespeare himself. This manuscript may give us a uniquely privileged glimpse into Shakespeare's creative process, making us feel we are almost present at the moment of writing. The process it reveals, however, is not that of a lonely genius sitting in his garret in London, summoning immortal characters and burning speeches from his imagination and sealing them onto parchment in a moment of inspired creativity. It shows us a working playwright, paid as part of a team to do some tinkering with an old script and hopefully get it into a shape that might keep the punters happy. If Hand D is indeed Shakespeare's, it offers a glimpse of Shakespeare doing the unglamorous work of a theatre professional, playing a skilled part of the entertainment industry's play-making process alongside his colleagues.

Thus various theatrical documents, when collected into the First Folio, were transformed into the authorial canon of Shakespeare. In fact, we could say that this book created the authorial figure of Shakespeare through the act of ascribing the plays to him. As John Jowett remarks, the First Folio firmly established the idea of a Shakespeare canon, with its author's picture opposite the title page, "isolating him from the theatre" and presenting poems by other writers in praise of his talent. The book advertised the "True Originall Copies", casting doubt on earlier quarto printings and implying that "nothing stood in between Shakespeare's pen and the text" (88-9). It also categorised the plays into "Comedies", "Tragedies" and "Histories", imposing a genre-based literary scheme in ways that jumbled up the order in which they been written and first appeared in the theatre, as well as changing some titles to fit the new divisions (Jowett, 89). In the First Folio we can see the idea of a Shakespeare canon emerging, centred around the individual talent of one writer and ignoring the other people he collaborated with in the theatre industry. We should also note that it did not include *Pericles* or *The Two Noble Kinsmen*, which are now firmly within the canon. When the former did appear in a later Folio, in the 1660s, it was accompanied by other new additions (such as *Locrine* and *1 Sir John Oldcastle*) which modern scholars do not consider to be by Shakespeare, whilst the latter had to wait until the twentieth century to be generally included in the canon.

So though the criterion for entry into the Shakespeare canon was fairly simple – the play had to be written by Shakespeare – the notion of authorship that underpins it becomes a lot more complex on closer inspection. We can be reasonably sure that the majority of plays with Shakespeare's name attached were by him, but the early modern period's notion of what that meant differs considerably from ours. Playwrights were part of a collaborative process that frequently involved working on different parts of the same play, using a plot drawn up by someone else, and creating roles to suit the particular skills and reputation of star actors. Given that Shakespeare had a long-term working relationship with an actor and manager like Richard Burbage, for whom he wrote Hamlet, Lear and Richard III, how much sense can it make to view these characters as entirely his own invention? When we have different versions of plays with passages that appear to have been rewritten or adapted for particular occasions and different staging conditions, how can we identify what Shakespeare "really meant" and what was his genius compromising with the conditions of the industry? Neither the way in which he authored the plays, nor the versions in which they reached the First Folio, allow us to identify *The Collected Works of Shakespeare* as the precise words that Shakespeare actually wrote without some hedging or hesitation.

In or Out: Apocryphal Books

As we have seen, the development of the books we know as the Bible and the works of Shakespeare involved ruling some works as inauthentic, unsuitable, fraudulent or simply not authoritative enough. Understanding the historical process can help us see the collections more clearly and appreciate the way our reading of them has been shaped by their past. We can also examine some of the excluded works, to consider why *The London Prodigal* or *The Shepherd of Hermas* might have appeared possible contenders for inclusion, and why they did not end up within the officially recognised covers. Here I'd like to look at two "apocryphal" books, both of which have caused considerable controversy during the last century and which some people argue should be included in the canon, or at least be recognised as containing authentic material. These are the Gospel of Thomas and *Double Falsehood*. As I will suggest, by examining these "dubious" or questionable books, we can clarify our thinking on what makes a work canonical, but we may also find that our assumptions about the canonical books are undermined. I have chosen *Double Falsehood* and the Gospel of Thomas because it is so difficult to produce a set of rules that exclude these works from the official collections, without calling into question some of the traditionally recognised works.

Secret Teachings from the Desert

The Gospel of Thomas is one of the so-called "Nag Hammadi library", a group of manuscripts whose discovery in the mid-twentieth century provoked great scholarly excitement and a

general public debate about the shape of the Bible.[1] The works
were discovered by accident in the 1940s by agricultural workers in
Egypt, and have been dated to the late fourth century. They appear
to contain the writings of Gnostic Christians, who believed in a
rigid split between spirit and body, and that the aim of religious
devotion was to escape the soul's entrapment in the material
universe (though debate continues over how precisely "Gnosticism"
existed as a belief system in the Ancient World). The Gospel of
Thomas had been known to exist from references in other ancient
manuscripts, but it had been thought lost forever. It does not take
the form we are familiar with from the canonical Gospels: there is
no narrative of Jesus' birth, ministry, controversies with religious
authorities or death and resurrection. Instead it contains a series
of sayings by Jesus, which the opening of the book declares were
spoken secretly to the apostles and recorded by Didymos Judas
Thomas. It promises that anyone who can comprehend the real
meaning of them, or "find the interpretation of these sayings", will
receive eternal life. The form of the Gospel of Thomas thus diverges
from those of Matthew, Mark, Luke and John, concentrating upon
hidden wisdom rather than public preaching or sacrificial death. This
fits with the outlines of Gnostic belief, since that religious tradition
would logically have very little interest in the life and activities of
the earthly (or historical) Jesus. Believing that the physical world
was evil and meaningless, and that the point of religious teaching
was to enable each human spirit to escape it, they would be more
interested in secret teachings than biography.

The Gospel of Thomas contains a number of sayings that will be
entirely familiar to modern Christians. A good example is number
nine:

> Jesus said, "Now the sower went out, took a handful (of seeds)
> and scattered them. Some fell on the road; the birds came and
> gathered them up. Others fell on rock, did not take root in the
> soil, and did not produce ears. And others well on thorns; they
> choked the seed(s) and worms ate them. And others fell on the
> good soil and it produced good fruit: it bore sixty per measure
> and a hundred and twenty per measure."
>
> (9)

---

1. Their impact continues to reverberate, not least in the fact that the title of
   an episode of the TV show *Gilmore Girls* contains a joke about the Nag
   Hammadi manuscripts.

There are equivalent versions of other familiar images from the canonical Gospels: the kingdom of God appears as a mustard seed, people need to take the beam out of their own eye before helping their brother take the mote out of his, the wicked tenants of a vineyard kill the owner's son, a shepherd loses one sheep and leaves ninety-nine others whilst he searches for it, and only fools put new wine into an old wineskin. There are also sayings that look unfamiliar in their particular form, but that draw on recognisable language, or express similar ideas, such as number four:

> Jesus said, "The man old in days will not hesitate to ask a small child seven days old about the place of life, and he will live. For many who are first will become last, and they will become one and the same."
>
> (4)

Whilst the form is unusual, this clearly brings together two ideas present in the better-known Gospels: that entering the kingdom requires being like a small child, and that "the last shall be first". Of course, combining these images or phrases in this way may slightly change their meaning, or at least encourage readers to see them in a different light, but the saying is built from elements that can be found in the canonical accounts of Jesus. There are also sayings that diverge noticeably from the major Gospels, such as number eighty-seven: "Jesus said 'Wretched is the body that is dependent upon a body, and wretched is the soul that is dependent upon these two'"; and number eleven:

> Jesus said, "This heaven will pass away, and the one above it will pass away. The dead are not alive, and the living will not die. In the days when you consumed what is dead, you made it what is alive. When you come to dwell in the light, what will you do? One the day when you were one you became two. But when you become two, what will you do?"

Some of the sayings begin with familiar material, but take a distinct turn towards the unexpected, such as number twenty-two:

> Jesus saw infants being suckled. He said to his disciples, "These infants being suckled are like those who enter the kingdom."
>
> They said to him, "Shall we then, as children, enter the kingdom?"
>
> Jesus said to them, "When you make the two one, and when you make the inside like the outside and the outside like the

inside, and the above like the below, and when you make the
male and female one and the same, so that the male not be
male nor the female female; and when you fashion eyes in
place of an eye, and a hand in place of a hand, and a foot in
place of a foot, and a likeness in place of a likeness, then will
you enter [the kingdom]."

Despite the shared imagery of children entering the kingdom,
this saying moves swiftly into distinctive language about "the two"
and "the one" which emphasises the division between the physical
and spiritual worlds in the religious systems influenced by Gnostic
thought. These are the moments at which the Gospel of Thomas
seems furthest away from orthodox Christianity, or at least the
documents that were canonised as the Bible.

So on examination, this apocryphal Gospel shares a great deal
of imagery and teaching with the more canonical books, but also
presents distinctively different ideas, both in familiar and unfamiliar
imagery. The overall form of the Gospel signals its unusual status,
since it ignores Jesus' life in favour of relating secret teachings which
are not embedded in any narratives that could explain their origins
or provide additional context to help readers towards their precise
meanings. This is certainly a serious contrast to the Gospels to be
found in the Bible, all of which contain a narrative of Jesus' suffering,
death and resurrection, and which present this as a major element in
the meaning that readers should take from the narratives about him.

On the other hand, there is considerable variation between the
canonical Gospels. John, for example, has no birth narrative, no
account of a Eucharist at the Last Supper, and records Jesus being
crucified on a different day. Only Matthew and Luke have the
Beatitudes or the Lord's Prayer, and only Matthew includes the flight
into Egypt. These are quite significant elements of the image of Jesus
and his teaching that Christians revere, and the distinctions between
the Gospels are often blurred by familiarity. Since most churches
and Christian communities treat the Gospels as a collective account
of Jesus' life and ministry, there is usually not much notice paid in
everyday practice to the fact that they present different information
and even rather different theology. When the Gospels are read in
church, for example, the name of the book is announced, but a large
proportion of the congregation probably do not mentally note that
this is the version of this healing story given in Mark, as opposed
to its variant in Matthew. Particularly for Christians who have been

brought up within the religion, and so heard simplified Bible stories during their childhood, at Sunday School or in children's groups, the various accounts of Jesus can blur into a general composite story. They remember that Jesus washed his disciples' feet, and commanded them to imitate his celebration of the Last Supper, and forgave the woman taken in adultery, and fed the five thousand, and gave a Sermon on the Mount, and drove the money-changers out of the Temple, and was born in Bethlehem, and was hidden in Egypt, and was tempted by the devil in the wilderness, and was mistaken for a gardener after his resurrection, and appeared on the road to Emmaus. These events are not only presented in the different Gospels (sometimes overlapping each other and sometimes not) but they are part of narratives that paint varying pictures of Jesus' identity and significance. The Jesus in Mark who insists that no-one talk about the miracles he performs, and who tries to ensure no-one recognises him as the Son of God, is a rather different figure from the Jesus in John who performs miracles as deliberate signs and wonders for people to see. The theology of John, in particular, when extracted from the other three, shows distinct similarities with the Gnostic ideas to be found within the Gospel of Thomas, with their joint emphasis on Jesus as a heavenly figure who belongs to another world, and who came into the earthly realm to help humans escape with him. It would hardly be a surprise to find the Jesus from the Gospel of Thomas declaring that "The Spirit gives life; the flesh counts for nothing", though those words actually originate in the sixth chapter of John.

It is worth remembering this as we read the apocryphal Gospels such as Thomas, and bearing in mind how much familiarity has smoothed over the strangeness and even inconsistency within the accepted canonical Gospels. Though there are definite differences between the forms of the Christian faith that the apocryphal documents present and the orthodox religion that centres around the canonical Bible, they would certainly seem less bizarre and wacky if they had been subjected to two millennia of theological commentary and harmonising with the other Biblical books.

A Quixotic Story of a Lost Cousin

If the Gospel of Thomas, as discussed above, provides a notable example of an apocryphal work that many scholars agree has some relevance to the canonical Biblical books, then the play entitled *Double Falsehood* gives us an example on the Shakespeare side. The discovery of a "lost play" by Shakespeare (or rather, that an existing known play might actually be a "lost play" under another title) must be a dream for many historians and scholars, but in the real world such a discovery is hedged about by complications and uncertainties. As we will see, there was no dusty manuscript discovered with the longed-for signature of "Wm Shakespeare", and no complete work which only had to be authenticated as genuine to be accepted as an entirely new and unknown play by Shakespeare's hand. The story is much more involved, more intriguing, and involves more disagreements about what exactly constitutes a play "by Shakespeare".

The Shakespeare canon has long looked to be incomplete, based on some fairly clear external evidence: there is a definite historical record of what seems to be a missing Shakespeare play.[1] Court records show performances of a play called *Cardenno* (or *Cardenna*) in the early 1610s, and in 1653 the publisher Humphrey Moseley recorded a work, in the official Stationers Register of books to be published, under the title *The History of Cardenio. by Mr. Fletcher. & Shakespeare*. Nearly a hundred years later, a play called *Double Falsehood* appeared on the London stage in 1727, advertised in the newspapers as "an original play by WILLIAM SHAKESPEARE", and appearing under the auspices of Lewis Theobald, who later produced an edition of Shakespeare. When Theobald published the play in 1728, he included a preface in which he insisted it was a genuine work by Shakespeare, stating that he possessed three copies of the play in manuscript, and saying he had been told that Shakespeare wrote it after he had retired to the country, as a present for his illegitimate daughter. (No such daughter is part of the Shakespeare mythology, as far as we know, adding another unusual touch to this story.) He tells his readers that the manuscripts are not all equally accurate, but that one of them is in the handwriting of Mr. Downes, who was the prompter of one of the theatre companies started in the 1660s, after the Civil War. Since Shakespeare died in 1616, this does not seem to be a claim that the copy dated back to his time, but perhaps an assurance that earlier figures in theatrical tradition, who knew people who could remember the pre-Civil War theatre, regarded this play as

---

1. An account of the play's history and possible transmission is given by Brean Hammond in the introduction to his edition of *Double Falsehood*, published in the Arden Shakespeare series. A rather more sceptical account is provided by Tiffany Stern, in her article "The Forgery of Some Modern Author?: Theobald's Shakespeare and Cardenio's Double Falsehood".

authentic. It is noticeable that Theobald himself does not claim to have found a single long-forgotten manuscript which preserves perfectly an unknown work by the master playwright, but suggests that there are surviving documents that can give us access to this work. It's also intriguing that, although he says that the play was written after Shakespeare had left London and retired to Stratford-upon-Avon, one of his copies is guaranteed by its connection to a theatre company fifty years later: Shakespeare is still a figure of the working theatre for Theobald, not entirely an isolated genius.

One certain fact about *Double Falsehood* is the absence now of the papers in which Theobald said he found the play. Whatever the truth about his claims to have collected the manuscripts of a lost Shakespeare work, all modern scholars have to go on is the text of the play as he printed it. There are a few possibilities, then. Firstly, it was all a complete hoax. Theobald, who was steeped in Shakespeare's language from his study of the playwright's works, decided to write the missing play and passed it off as a lost masterpiece. Secondly, there were one or more old manuscripts which Theobald worked from in putting together this play. If this is the case, there are still several unanswered questions: did Theobald correctly believe them to be by Shakespeare? Did he incorrectly believe them to be by Shakespeare? Did he believe they contained some Shakespearean material that he could "rescue" by writing pseudo-Shakespearean verse around the authentic material?[1] Bearing in mind the drastic way in which the post-Civil War theatre adapted and rewrote Shakespearean plays (which will be discussed in more detail in the next chapter), there is also the chance that Theobald was working from a radical rewrite of a Shakespearean original. Thirdly, it is all true and Theobald knew himself to be working from authentic Shakespearean materials, which he scrupulously pieced together into the best possible text of the lost play *Cardenio*. Whatever the truth, we also have to bear in mind that the text we have passed through Theobald, one of the major figures in the history of Shakespearean editions, but one who did not necessarily share all our assumptions about Shakespeare. We will never know for certain

---

1. There is one more permutation of these questions, which is logically possible but deeply improbable: did Theobald believe they were not by Shakespeare, when they actually were? The notion of Theobald deciding to hash up a fake Shakespeare play about Cardenio from manuscripts that happened to preserve a genuine play by Shakespeare is entertaining, but surely beyond the realms of reasonable speculation.

how he treated the manuscripts (if they existed), what changes he made to them based upon his sense of what real Shakespearean verse should sound like, and to what extent they might have already contained the changes made by earlier adapters or performers.

As well as offering us a potential lost play to read, stage and enjoy, an apocryphal work like *Double Falsehood* challenges us to think about what we mean by "a Shakespeare play". Can we only call it that if we possess a manuscript in the author's handwriting? In that case, we don't have any plays by Shakespeare. Is it a play that we are sure was only written by Shakespeare, and contains no influences or contributions from anyone else? Given the way Shakespeare worked, writing for an established company of actors with their own particular skills, some of whom were skilled improvisers, this would also require us to discard the existing canon. Can we describe a play as "by Shakespeare" if he was the only playwright who worked on it, even though actors and printers might have left their mark on it? In this case serious chunks of the Complete Works will have to be jettisoned. We would certainly lose *The Two Noble Kinsmen* and *Pericles*, probably *Titus Andronicus* and *1 Henry VI*, maybe *Timon of Athens*, and if we were being strict, even *Measure for Measure* and *Macbeth* would have to go. Shakespeare's apparent collaborations include some less-performed works, but also plays that are absolutely central to the modern repertory and to our sense of him as a distinctive creative artist. Despite the complex and uncertain history of *Double Falsehood*, there is no easy definition we can impose that would rule it out and maintain the existing canon as it stands.

Apocrypha and Their (Dubious) Influence

The two apocryphal works we have examined – *Double Falsehood* and the Coptic Gospel of Thomas – can offer us several things. Most obviously, they may contain authentic material that extends the boundaries of Shakespeare and the Bible, if only by a very small amount. Neither satisfies the popular image of a miraculous manuscript that pre-dates all our existing sources, redefining what we should think about Christianity or Shakespearean theatre by offering us a privileged glimpse into the very earliest days of each. On the contrary, they appear to be substantially later sources that may nonetheless preserve material lost in the transmission process that produced our current canon. There may be sayings of Jesus and poetry by Shakespeare that we have never heard before in these documents, but in order to find them we have to undertake painstaking textual analysis. This very frustration also offers us something. The fact that there is no newsflash from the distant past in these books, no magic voice calling out the truth above the white noise of history, reminds us of the historical processes that gave rise to our existing canons. The activity of taking apart the Gospel of Thomas, or plotting the potential connections between *Double Falsehood* and the lost *Cardenio*, should highlight the contingent status of the texts we are used to thinking of as secure. All our "sacred texts" are subject to the same historical confusions, and everything we hear in them is mediated by centuries of copying, interpretation and controversy. It is useful to be reminded of this.

The slight extension of the authoritative collection that each work might offer is worth considering seriously. If these apocrypha do preserve some genuine material, then it should interest us beyond the excitement provided by reading more of what we've been used to. Each text has the potential to shift the emphasis of the existing canon, if only very subtly. If the picture of Jesus presented in the Gospel of Thomas is accepted as (partially) based on authentic traditions then it might emphasise his status as a teacher of paradoxical epigrams and "hard sayings" (to quote John's Gospel). It could move attention away from his sacrificial death and towards his spiritual insights; away from a simple demand for belief and towards the insistent mysteries of the kingdom. Likewise, if *Double Falsehood* has transmitted material from a genuine Shakespearean original, it could nuance the outlines of his image. A Shakespeare who was conversant with Continental literature to the extent of writing a play based on an episode from Cervantes is not the popularly recognised figure. The Shakespeare who wrote *Henry V* and is quoted by belligerent politicians criticising Europe might have to contend with a Shakespeare who could be comfortably regarded as a European intellectual. Neither of these images – of Jesus and of Shakespeare – are absent from the existing canon, but these apocryphal works would shift the outlines just a little in their favour. Finally, *Double Falsehood* and the Coptic Gospel of Thomas offer us a helpful challenge by demanding that we define what "a Gospel" and "a Shakespeare play" mean. Whether we produce those definitions in order to rule them in or out, when we grapple with this doubtful but exciting material we are forced to clarify our ideas about the existing texts within the canon. This helps us think more precisely about the works we assume we know, and causes us to see them from another angle. The obvious weirdness and improbability of the apocrypha can alert us again to the weirdness and improbability we so often gloss over in the canon.

(In)conclusions about Canons

This chapter has covered a great deal of historical and conceptual ground, necessarily condensing and simplifying complex matters in order to provide a broad outline. Perhaps the most significant insight to be gained by looking at the history of the canon of both Shakespeare and the Bible is the most basic one: these canons both have a history. The cultural weight and authority these books carry can sometimes trick us into thinking that they have always existed, and have always been in the form they take now. A historical perspective disrupts this illusion, and allows us to notice the practical, contingent and even accidental events that helped to shape the versions we have today. It allows us to critically observe the principles upon which decisions were made, and also enables us to speculate on what might have happened if events had gone in a different direction. Perhaps most importantly, it reveals the way in which the canon itself is an idea that has shifted its meaning over time. From the "open" and "closed" canonicity of Christian Scriptures to the use of Shakespeare's name by the quartos and Folios, this chapter has shown that we can risk serious misunderstanding if we project our own understanding of the canon back into the past. It may be glib to point out that everyone in the past wasn't busy trying to become us, but it is nonetheless worth bearing that fact in mind. We need to be alert to the shifts in the idea of the canon itself, as well as its contents, if we are to understand the history of these books.

There are a few other general insights that this chapter has offered, alongside the historical details. Both books are the result of a process of critical and careful reading: the decisions on which documents should be included or excluded were not simply based upon external factors like the appearance of a manuscript or the name of a writer. The canons emerged after people were already reading the texts, not as a pre-condition for that reading. Connected to this is the insight that both books emerged from groups of people engaged in specific and unusual activities: the Christian communities and the London theatres. They were the results of shared artistic and spiritual lives, as well as being subject to all the personal influences, disagreements and power politics that human communities involve. The collections we now have were produced for certain ends, whether to make money or to make disciples, and those ends will have influenced the shape of the collection. Having surveyed the history of the canon, I will now investigate a topic that has only been touched on briefly so far, by looking at the words within those books. Exploring the canon may have challenged some assumptions about what is meant by the phrase "Shakespeare and the Bible"; investigating the problems with determining their texts may call some more into question.

2.
The Text Itself (II):
The Words on the Page

Having discussed which works might be included in the canon, I would like to raise another foundational issue: what words are included in those works. So far I have been discussing the plays of Shakespeare and the books of the Bible as if they were entirely stable collections of words which could be moved around within the canon, secure that there was no disagreement over the texts themselves. This, however, is not the case. We do not possess the original works, whatever form they might have taken; instead, we possess a set of books and manuscripts of those works. Crucially, not all of those books and manuscripts even agree on the exact wording of the text. The study of how these differences relate to each other, and to the work itself, is the discipline of textual criticism.

The New Testament and Its Text(s)

Scholars wishing to establish the best text possible of the New Testament are faced with an array of manuscripts, many displaying slight variations in the text.[1] Overall, the texts are relatively stable, and something approaching ninety-five per cent of the New Testament is not in question. However, given the respect and attention that people lavish on the NT, and the authority it is accorded, even five per cent of instability is significant. This is, after all, not five per cent of disagreement on the precise meaning of the words involved, let alone what their implications should be for those involved in Christian churches. It is five percent of variability in the words

---

1. I will focus on the New Testament in this chapter, as I did in the chapter on canonical questions, since it is later in date and there are more manuscripts available for us to consult. This means the textual criticism of the New Testament has more in common with the equivalent techniques applied to Shakespeare.

themselves, and some of the passages in doubt have potentially dramatic consequences for those who consider the Bible to have religious authority. As we will see, attitudes to adultery, forgiveness, the Trinity and the identity of Christ are all potentially affected by the issues raised by textual criticism. However, before considering individual variations in the text, it is worth looking at the origins of those differences: the surviving manuscripts.

The Manuscripts of the New Testament (and Proper Joined-Up Writing)

There are approximately five thousand manuscripts of the NT surviving today in the original Greek, although that does not mean five thousand complete copies. Only about sixty are complete New Testaments, and the vast majority are fragmentary, some containing a few lines or even just a few words. About a hundred are written on papyrus, with the remainder on parchment. The earlier manuscripts tend to be written in capital letters without spaces between words (which makes deciphering them something of a skill), with lower-case writing and spaces becoming more generally used in the later copies. Calling them "manuscripts" obscures both the variety of sizes and shapes in which they come – from scrappy fragments of papyrus to elaborately decorated volumes written in silver and gold ink on purple vellum – and also the different purposes that they appear to have served. The major manuscripts include "continuous" text, which is what we would usually think of as a copy of the NT or the Biblical book, and "lectionaries", which are collections of passages designed to be read out on the particular days of the Christian calendar. This is complicated further by other, less obvious, uses to which texts appears to have been put: copied into amulets, for example, or used for fortune-telling or other magical activities. As David C. Parker points out, "there are inconsistencies between the inclusion and exclusion" of papyrus fragments on these grounds, never mind the problems posed by "manuscripts" that are, in fact, shards of pottery (32-57). There are further pieces of evidence for lost versions of particular texts, such as quotations from the group of bishops and theologians from the early centuries of Christianity who have become known as the Church Fathers. If a quotation from the NT turns up in one of their theological treatises, and does not correspond to a version of the text which survives, it may be that their work has preserved a variant reading that existed at the time but has subsequently been lost. This is not as strong evidence as an actual manuscript (or a fragment of one) that includes that variation, since there are various reasons why the treatise might not have preserved an actual version which existed. The writer might have been quoting from memory and got the wording slightly wrong, or might have been adapting the line to make a point, expecting the reader to see the difference between the Biblical version and his adaptation. He might even be adjusting the quotation slightly without expecting his readers to know that he had done so, because the new version supported the theological argument he was making. These need to be treated with some caution. However, they do count as potential "witnesses" to textual versions that have been lost over the centuries since.

Having collected and catalogued the existing manuscripts and witnesses to the text (which is a mammoth task in itself), textual criticism involves trying to categorise them into "families" or "groups". This is based upon the principle that all manuscripts were copied from a previous one, so if we had all the necessary information there is a theoretical "family tree" of manuscripts to be written, showing which older manuscripts gave rise to which later ones. This also assumes that the majority of textual differences entered the family tree at one specific point, when a scribe accidentally or deliberately made a change whilst copying. Therefore manuscripts "above" that point in the family tree will not include that difference, whereas manuscripts "below" that point, which are "descended" from that manuscript, will show that difference. Manuscripts that are later in date, but which are not descended from the manuscript in which that change was made, will also not include that difference in their version of the text. One way to imagine this is as a genetic mutation which suddenly occurred in one member of a family, for one of the various reasons beloved of sci-fi fans, perhaps involving the action of aliens, or of an experimental attempt to create a super-hero gone wrong.[1] Any children that person had subsequently would carry those mutated genes, as would their grandchildren and so on. However, their nephews and nieces would not, since they carried genes that had not been affected by the event that caused the mutation. We are in the position of only having the genetic material, and having to

---

1. I should at this point add a disclaimer to the effect that my knowledge of modern science fiction is lacking in some details, although it is by no means as abject as my knowledge of the science of genetics. I hope this will not affect the analogy for those readers who are more conversant in these fields.

work back logically to deduce that the mutation occurred. Except that the mutation is a different word ending, or a missing clause, and there are several thousand of them in the same genetic code, all of which presumably entered the family gene pool at different points. In order to aid the sorting process, we have some external information such as the age of the manuscript, the place where it was found, its physical appearance and condition, and so on. With this external information, and the internal contents of the texts, some conclusions can be cautiously drawn about the connections between the surviving manuscripts.

Scholars disagree on how useful it is to put manuscripts into "families" like this. Some would argue that we can only propose a particular textual variant as "correct" on the basis of an argument about which manuscripts display it and how far back it can be argued to go. The manuscripts and their comparative differences are the only hard data available to us, they would suggest, and they provide a check against the tendency of scholars to prefer one variant over another because of their personal aesthetic preferences, or theological opinions. There is also an argument made that grouping manuscripts into families can help clear up misconceptions about how widespread certain variations are. If two manuscripts disagree about a particular word, and one shares its variant with six manuscripts, whilst the other shares its variant with seventy, it might seem reasonable to prefer the more widespread version. The six look like an aberration compared to the balance of evidence in the seventy. However, if all of those seventy came from one family of manuscripts, and the six from widely differing families, they would in fact be evidence of a more widespread version.

On the other hand, a number of scholars are extremely sceptical about our ability to reconstruct family trees, or even family groups, effectively and accurately. Bruce Metzger has questioned whether the methods of comparison that are used to produce the theories are sufficiently robust, and whether critics take into account the fact that manuscripts which agree with each other may do so by chance rather than by family connection (181). Keith Elliott and Ian Moir note that "only a very small proportion of the larger number of extent manuscripts can be shown to be copies of ones that we already have", and that therefore "the majority of NT manuscripts do not seem to be members of families at all", concluding that the "genealogical method" of searching for the original text is "a non-starter" (23-24). These criticisms generally rest on the idea that we simply do not have enough historical evidence to draw solid conclusions about the family relationships between manuscripts. They assert that it can be a useful way to imagine the descent of the text that gave rise to the manuscripts we possess today, but the more historical evidence we discover, the more we discover that we do not know.

Cross-Examining the Witnesses

However the surviving manuscripts relate to each other, there are differences between them that are significant enough to need some way of reconciling them. It is sometimes suggested by popular books on the Bible, and some more conservative textbooks, that textual criticism is a fuss about nothing. Daniel B. Wallace suggests that "no cardinal doctrine, no essential truth, is affected by any viable variant in the surviving New Testament manuscripts" (in Grudem et al). Even if it were true that no major Christian ideas are called into question by textual variants (and I think that is far from proven), a lot of Christian readers regard the Bible as much more than a few doctrines generally expressed in more or less suitable words. They certainly treat it in ways that suggest that the words themselves are extremely important and valuable. Textual criticism, and the issues it raises, has serious implications for the Christian use of the Bible. Probably the most striking cases raised by textual study are the passages that appear in the manuscripts upon which Bibles were based in the English-speaking world before the nineteenth century, but which are missing from other manuscripts discovered since. The two manuscripts known as Vaticanus and Siniaticus, edited and published during the nineteenth century, are generally regarded as reliable and authoritative by textual scholars. In both of them, the Gospel of Mark ends at 16:8, instead of continuing on until 16:20. The importance of this is evident when the passage is consulted: it involves a young man meeting Mary Magdalene and her female companions at the empty tomb, and instructing them to tell Peter and the other disciples that Jesus would meet them all in Galilee:

> [8] So they went out and fled from the tomb, for terror and amazement had seized them; and they said nothing to anyone, for they were afraid.

In the two major manuscripts mentioned above, the Gospel ends here, although in the text upon which Western pre-nineteenth-century Bibles are based it continues with Jesus visiting Mary

Magdalene, appearing to other disciples, commissioning his followers to go out and proclaim the gospel, and then ascending to heaven. This is a significantly different ending to the narrative. Perhaps not in ways which affect central doctrines: Christ is reported as having risen, so this version of Mark does not leave us simply with the death of Jesus and the mourning of his disciples without at least mentioning the triumph over death which forms so central a part of the Christian narrative. The resurrection is detailed in the other Gospels, as are Jesus' appearances to the disciples and the sending out of the disciples to preach and act in his name, so to that extent this does not leave out material that is not supplied elsewhere. There is a very different tone, however, to a narrative that ends with only three disciples having heard about the resurrection, and with them not telling anyone about it because of their fear. It suspends the narrative that we are more used to from the other Gospels at a point before the triumphant confirmation of Jesus' continued life, before the institution of the church on earth, before the mourning for him is over, before the shadow of the tomb has been dispelled and replaced by the light and glory of the ascension. It may not miss out any crucial doctrine that can be extracted from the story and established as a theological principle, but this is a very different situation to end the story on. It alters the narrative shape of the whole Gospel, and leaves the readers in a different position as they follow the actions of the disciples left behind after the crucifixion. Given this discrepancy, scholars have carefully compared the final twelve verses with the rest of the book, and found that "language, style and theological content brand it as non-Markan", indicating that the ending was not written by the same author as the rest of the Gospel (Elliott and Moir, 40). However, the grammar of verse eight makes it unlikely that the narrative originally ended there, suggesting that there might well have been another ending which was altered or replaced with the better-known version. Given the age of the manuscripts that contain the longer ending, this must have happened at a relatively early point in Christian history. Thus the problem cannot quite be resolved by either excising the whole ending and claiming that verse eight is the real ending of the Gospel, nor by regarding verses nine to twenty as the original as it was written (or as it was circulated in the earliest decades of Christianity).

The story of the "woman taken in adultery", so well-known that it produced a proverb about "casting the first stone" which many people quote without knowing its Biblical source, is also missing from some early and reliable manuscripts. The episode is usually found in the Gospel of John, at the end of chapter seven and the beginning of chapter eight, though "there are at least five other locations" for it in existing manuscripts, and "there is a great deal of textual variety within the story itself", with "six or seven" variant versions. Like the ending of Mark, both the linguistic features and the literary style of the "woman taken in adultery" episode are different from the surrounding narrative, and Elliott and Moir conclude that "the story, famous and beloved though it is, is . . . no part of the original NT" (40). This episode matters less for the overall shape of the Gospel it appears in than the issue of Mark's ending, but is often referred to in modern Christian discussions of ethics. It is particularly cited in debates over sexuality and sexual activity, one of the most pressing issues facing Christian churches. Suggesting that it is not part of the New Testament is a meaningful change to the familiar stock of stories and sayings that guide Christian thought.

However, this conclusion does not mean the story must be dismissed altogether: though they exclude it from the verifiable text of the NT, Elliott and Moir believe that its multiple versions indicate it was "a piece of early floating Christian tradition" which became attached to various parts of the canonical works (40). Excluding it from the attempt to find the original text does not mean concluding that it was deliberately invented by an unscrupulous scribe, nor that it could not preserve some authentic memory of Jesus' ethical teachings. There is a shorter – but potentially more important – disagreement between manuscripts at 1 John 5:7-8. In the King James Bible, this reads:

[7] For there are three that bear record in heaven, the Father, the Word, and the Holy Ghost, and these three are one.
[8] And there are three that bear witness in earth, the Spirit, and the water, and the blood: and these three agree in one.

However, modern editions such as the New Revised Standard Version print the lines thus:

[7] There are three that testify: [8] the Spirit, and the water and the blood, and these three agree.

The longer version appears in some late Greek manuscripts, but appears to have originated in manuscripts of the Vulgate, the fourth-century Latin translation of the Bible. This is the most explicit reference to the doctrine of the Trinity in the New Testament;

the end of the Gospel of Matthew has Jesus instruct his disciples to baptise "in the name of the Father, and of the Son and of the Holy Spirit", but does not state that "these three are one". It is striking that the addition seems to have originated during the fourth century, the era when the doctrine of the Trinity was being officially established. This does not mean, however, that there was a deliberate attempt to falsify the document by adding in words to confirm a new doctrine. The words could have been a comment by a scribe to help readers understand what he took to be the real meaning of the passage; since such comments were often written between the lines as well as in the margins, the explanatory words could have been mistakenly incorporated into the text during later copying. It is even possible that the original author of the epistle did have an idea of God in mind that bore similarities to the eventual doctrine of the Trinity, and so the scribe's gloss was an accurate account of the lines' meaning. As the manuscripts stand, however, this addition has to be regarded – like the two previous examples – as a piece of Christian tradition that has shaped the understanding of the book, rather than part of the original text.

Most variants in the text are neither so large nor so dramatic as these few examples. Much of the work of textual criticism consists of comparing very small differences in the texts contained by the manuscripts, and making judgements as to which version should be preferred. These decisions are based on theories about what sort of mistakes or alterations are most likely during the transmission of the text. Some variants are explained on the basis of accidental errors by the scribe, such as the tendency of anyone copying out long passages of text to let their eye skip between lines that contain similar phrases. For example, one manuscript has Jesus stating in Mark 10:7, "And for this reason a man shall leave his father and his mother and the two shall become one".[1] This does not appear to make much sense when compared with the more familiar version: "And for this reason a man shall leave his father and his mother and unite with his wife and the two shall become one".[2] The variant can be explained in this case by the fact that in the original Greek the phrase "his and"

---

1. These examples follow the explanation of textual criticism in Elliott and Moir's *Manuscripts and the Text of the New Testament*.
2. Though without the more familiar and widely-attested version of Jesus' saying, it might suggest that the Jewish culture of the time was exempt from empty-nest syndrome and parents rather enjoyed having the place to themselves again after the children had left home for university.

appears at the beginning and the end of the portion of text that has been missed out. It is probable that the scribe's eye skipped between the two phrases and so the text in the middle was missed out. Two other examples of this kind of error are more obvious in English. I have highlighted the missing portion of text with italics:

> . . . but do not have love, *I have become a noisy gong or a clanging cymbal. And if I have prophetic powers, and understand all mysteries and all knowledge, and if I have all faith so as to remove mountains, but do not have love* I am nothing.
>
> (1 Corinthians 13:1-2)

> *And it was given to him to make war on the saints and conquer them.* And it was given to him to have authority . . .
>
> (Revelation 13:7)

Other variants appear to have been alterations on stylistic grounds. Elliott and Moir cite Mark 12:23, in which some manuscripts have "in the Resurrection" and others have "in the Resurrection, when they are raised". Though the latter has an "unnecessary clause", it is "typical of Mark's style" and likely to have been tidied up by later scribes who were better versed in sophisticated Greek rhetoric than the original author (48). Still other variants seem to be the result of judgements about the genre of a passage, such as Acts 15:20 and 29, which jointly warn Christians "to abstain from" four things: "things polluted by idols", "fornication", "blood" and "whatever has been strangled". Variations amongst the manuscripts include some that leave out the injunction against "whatever has been strangled" and some that leave out "fornication". As Elliott and Moir point out, these appear to be the result of different interpretations of the list of prohibitions. A list forbidding idol worship, the shedding of blood, and fornication appears to be a set of moral precepts to guide ethical behaviour. Prohibitions against food offered to idols, animals that have been strangled and blood products looks more like a set of ceremonial restrictions around diet. The variant versions seem to have been based on differing interpretations of the kind of instruction being given here, summed up in the ambiguity around the real meaning of the word "blood" in the verses. It is entirely possible that one set of scribes or the other were correct, and this is either a set of food guidelines or a summing-up of ethical precepts. Printing all four prohibitions leaves the ambiguity in place, but this seems to be the right solution based upon the textual evidence.

A host of textual variants can only be solved by close attention to the grammar of the original passage, the likelihood of change during transmission, the balance of probability that only one of four available variants could lead to all of the other three appearing as mistakes, and other technical issues. However, as the examples above show, textual criticism is not a scientific process that can take place before questions of meaning are involved. There is no way to establish the text definitively and certainly, based only upon external evidence from the manuscripts, before proceeding to read the text and reflect on its meaning. Literary style, theology, genre, and religious history are all involved in the process of establishing the best and most likely text. Bruce Metzger has remarked that "to teach another how to become a textual critic is like teaching another how to become a poet" (305). This is particularly the case in so-called "conjectural emendations", where a critic is faced with a text that seems not to make sense, but does not have an alternative reading provided by any of the available manuscripts. In this case, with caution and based upon their knowledge of religious, linguistic and generic context, scholars suggest what the text "should" read. These emendations are more typical of editing the Old Testament, where the textual witnesses are fewer and there is less likelihood of a variant reading to rectify what appears to be a mistaken line.

Shakespeare and the Texts of Shakespeare

Before discussing the history of textual criticism as applied to Shakespeare, it is worth noticing its prehistory.[1] In order for editors and scholars such as Pope, Malone and W.W. Greg to disagree on the precise text of Shakespeare's plays, a very basic condition needs to be in place: everyone needs to agree that the play is defined by the words it contains. This seems so basic as to not need stating, but it took something like two hundred years for this idea to emerge as the definition of a work by Shakespeare. Jean I. Marsden traces this shift in *The Re-Imagined Text*, which starts from the fact – startling to modern sensibilities – that theatres in the seventeenth and eighteenth centuries quite happily rewrote Shakespeare in what would seem to us drastic and even ridiculous ways. Nahum Tate famously rewrote *King Lear* so that it had a happy ending, an act that might appear to rather miss the point of one of the greatest tragedies

---

1. An alternative "prehistory" of Shakespeare and editing is provided by Sonia Massai in *Shakespeare and the Rise of the Editor*.

in the English language (even if it restored some aspects of the story in the sources that Shakespeare himself had used). John Dryden turned *The Tempest* into *The Tempest, or The Enchanted Island*, which altered much of the text and introduced new characters, including sisters for Caliban and Miranda and a romantic interest for Ariel. Though there have been famous adaptations of Shakespeare in the twentieth century, which make radical changes to the setting and language of the play – *West Side Story* and *Forbidden Planet*, for example – there is a difference between modern adaptations and the work of Tate and Dryden. They did not consider themselves to be radically changing Shakespeare's works, and would probably not have considered the resulting play to be an "adaptation" in our sense. They did not regard Shakespeare's plays as a set of texts that had been written once and for all, and which consisted of a specific sequence of words fixed on the page.

This does not mean that Shakespeare was regarded as valueless or disposable in the period that his works were being so broadly and deeply altered for theatrical performance. On the contrary, they held him in high esteem, though those who admired him did not assume that what they appreciated was necessarily located in the specific words of particular speeches; as Marsden puts it, "while they revered the poet, did not revere his language *per se*" (2). Dryden, himself both a critic and a poet, was quite happy to make this belief explicit, when he wrote that "words are not like landmarks, so sacred as never to be removed" (in Marsden, 2). It is telling, perhaps, that when we use the word "Shakespeare" in casual conversation, in phrases such as "I'm a big fan of Shakespeare" or "There's quite a lot of Shakespeare to see in London this season", it's not always clear in what sense precisely we are using the word. "Shakespeare" seems to stand for both a specific person in the past, the person regarded as the author of some plays, and the body of work as a whole. It also refers to a whole cultural phenomenon: "Shakespeare" has come to connote much more than an author or a collection of literature, though that will be explored in a later chapter. The very uncertainty over whether the phrase "oh, no, not another college course on Shakespeare!" is using the word to mean a person or a set of writings shows how easily we elide the gap between these two meanings. It highlights the extent to which Shakespeare the writer and Shakespeare the words have become inextricably linked for us, in a way that only solidified in the eighteenth century. In Marsden's phrase, "Shakespeare as author also becomes Shakespeare as document" (4).

The move to a documentary or textual Shakespeare had profound implications for the ways in which the works were discussed, reproduced and imagined. Marsden has traced the shift from a Shakespeare criticism that was concerned with "the manipulation of the audience's response to a visual and audible representation" to one that "stressed the interplay among author, text, and reader" (127). In her account this went along with changes from a mode of aesthetic appreciation that focused on common rationality, consensus and sociable responses to one that emphasised the subjective engagement of each person's attention and emotional interaction with the text. With the work identified as a specific sequence of words, there was less concern with elements like plot or the overall impression of the play, and more attention was paid to individual speeches and verbal clues to meaning. Other chapters will investigate further how this conception of Shakespeare as a text led to particular interpretative styles and practices, but it is important to notice that it was a serious shift in how the plays had been conceptualised. What may appear so basic as not to even be worth saying for us – that the works of Shakespeare are certain particular words arranged in long sequences, and are fixed as those words in that order – was not always the case, and came about as part of the history of Shakespeare. By this point, readers may not be surprised to hear Marsden using religious language to describe the situation that came about in the eighteenth century: she suggests that "[t]oday the idea of changing Shakespeare's words seems blasphemous" and speaks generally of the "reverence" paid to the author and his works (1). For her, the move to a textual conception of Shakespeare put in place the conditions necessary for Shakespeare's text to be regarded and treated "as a sacred object, a kind of secular bible" (127).

Once this stage had been reached, and Shakespeare was thoroughly identified with the text, there was a series of major editors who attempted to "restore" errors in the text, using approaches that had been developed for Classical and Biblical texts. This was in itself proof of the high status that Shakespeare was acquiring, since it involved placing him alongside the great authors of Greek and Roman culture and the religious texts of the Christian tradition, at least in terms of the attention paid to his texts and the techniques applied to them. From the eighteenth century onwards, a series of major editions were produced, creating a sense that there was an "authorised" text of Shakespeare in the making, even if it was contested. (The idea that new editions of Shakespeare provided a better text each time was also extremely beneficial to the publishers.) Some of this work was carried out by figures who are mostly remembered today for their Shakespeare editions, such as Lewis Theobald, Edward Capell and Edmund Malone, but Samuel Johnson and Alexander Pope also produced significant editions. When a modern editor produces an edition, they implicitly or explicitly place themselves in this line of succession, often by including notes on their text as to which of the previous textual alterations they have followed. Since Capell was the first editor to work on the principle that the earliest copies will be the most useful in establishing the correct text, later editors are implicitly claiming to both move the editorial project further forward (by improving on the texts presented by previous editors) and to offer a text that is older (by restoring elements from an imagined earlier text).

The process of editing a Shakespeare play follows some similar principles to editing a Biblical text, though the materials are somewhat different. Since there are many fewer sources from which to edit a Shakespearean text, they are all printed books, and they are much more recent, there is a much better chance of producing a coherent account of the descent of a particular text. We can, for example, discover a certain amount about the careers and habits of particular publishers and booksellers, and even a few of the scribes who worked for the theatre companies. This means that Shakespeare editors are even more invested in producing narratives for their editorial choices than Biblical scholars. They may decide to adopt one reading over another because they believe they can detect a particular stylistic quirk of a scribe, or the compositor who set the printed letters. They may prefer one version of a line over another because we know that in 1606 the Act to Restrain the Abuses of Players led to the replacement of God's name in oaths performed onstage, or because they suspect one text is based on an earlier draft of the same speech. We have much more information about the conditions of production, and the individual people involved, in the early Shakespeare texts than in the early New Testament texts, so there is more corroborative evidence to confirm or disprove a particular theory. This ties the process of editing even more closely to the process of reading, interpreting and speculating about the creation of the versions that have survived. Though there is more evidence available about the technical features of the printed books, editors still proceed by trying to make sense of the text they have received, and resorting to narratives to explain apparently nonsensical or improbable lines.

Due to the shorter chain of transmission, many editions of Shakespeare by publishers like Arden or Oxford provide a "critical apparatus" alongside the play, in which they note variations from the text they have printed. These can vary from significant differences to minor issues of punctuation or spelling, and can also refer to the changes made by previous editors. For example, the Arden edition of *The Tempest* prints Act 2, Scene 1, Line 164 as "Of its own kind all foison, all abundance", with a note at the bottom of the page which reads "164 its] *F4;* it *F;* its' *F3.*" This informs the reader that the word "its" appears in the fourth version of the Folio in the form printed, but that the first Folio prints "it" and the third Folio prints "its'". The same edition prints line 220 of the same scene as "Trebles thee o'er", with the note "221 Trebles . . . o'er] Troubles . . . o'er *Rowe*; Troubles . . . not *Hanmer*; Trembles . . . o'er *Johnson*". This records the versions printed by the editors named, which all change the meaning of the line significantly. Sometimes editors are forced into the sort of conjectural emendation I mentioned above, with one particularly famous example appearing in the description of Falstaff's death in Act 2, Scene 3 of *Henry V*. In the Folio text, Mistress Quickly recounts the dying knight's appearance, saying that "his nose was as sharp as a pen, and a table of green fields". This somewhat baffling comparison was emended by Lewis Theobald in the 1730s to "a [he] babbled of green fields", imagining Falstaff deliriously remembering pastoral England as he passed away. There is no textual evidence for this, besides the fact that the line as printed does not appear to make any sense, and there has been considerable scholarly debate over these green fields, as scholars from Samuel Johnson to Gary Taylor gave their opinions.

Emendations of this sort are inevitably controversial, since they involve declaring that part of a "sacred" text is nonsense and needs changing without any other manuscript or printed book to offer an alternative, or even corroborate that the existing text might be wrong. In this situation an editor may be accused of claiming that they know better than the author whose works have attracted such attention, or of wishing to make their own mark in a huge tradition of editing and commentary by a perverse alteration. Certainly conjectural emendations involve making a definite statement about the meaning (or lack of it) in a text in a way that apparently involves a value judgement on it. But they are only the most obvious and drastic example of what we have seen all the way through this examination of textual transmission and editing; every edition involves making decisions about meaning. They are all acts of interpretation, and all involve the conscientious and creative "reading" that is the central theme of this book.

Textual Criticism Peers Beyond the Text

If textual critics – as we have seen – aim to produce a better text from the surviving documents, they have to make certain assumptions about the relationships between the text as it exists now and past versions of it. The very practical activities of comparing manuscripts and books, noting discrepancies and constructing explanations, can obscure the fact that there is a whole set of theoretical presuppositions that underpin the search for a better text. These have been debated and questioned by scholars in both Shakespeare and Biblical Studies for as long as editing has been going on, and in the late twentieth century some critiques went as far as questioning the very possibility of an ideal text.

In Shakespeare Studies, the search for the ideal text was summed up by a movement known as the New Bibliography in the early twentieth century. Its major figures, such as Fredson Bowers and W.W. Greg, had a generally optimistic attitude towards the possibilities their work held, believing that a rigorous and scientific approach would eventually lead to the establishment of a good, or even effectively perfect, text for Shakespeare's works. In *Editing Shakespeare and the Elizabethan Dramatists*, Bowers declares that "the editorial ideal" is for a scholar to take a particular reliable version of the text, and make emendations in it from other sources in order to "recove[r] features of the lost original, giv[ing] them substantive being" and eventually leading to "the complete and pure wording of the original" (in McDonald, *Shakespeare*, 267). The entire enterprise of the New Bibliography may be said to have rested upon this belief: that careful critical work will genuinely result in the recovery of the precise wording of texts that have been corrupted, confused or obscured by centuries of printing and transcription. In Bowers' phrase, a "veil of print" exists between the scholar and the original manuscript, which it is their job to remove. This leads into the other sense in which the New Bibliography was "idealistic", since it was concerned to reconstruct a text of which there were no remaining copies. The process of emending a text based upon the suspicion of errors made by scribes, printers (and even the author themselves) was a declaration of faith in an ideal version of the literary work, which had to be deduced from the traces it left behind. In extreme form, this was a faith in a text that had never existed on paper, only having existence in the intentions of the author (or the scholar's deduction of those intentions). Though the New Bibliographers varied in the confidence with which they believed this quest could be carried out, and in their certainty of its being concluded successfully, their work depended upon a sense that it was, in theory, possible to recover lost originals from the texts that were available to readers hundreds of years later.

Leah Marcus' *Unediting the Renaissance*, published in the 1990s, mounted a sustained critique of the possibility of achieving the single pure edition dreamed of by the New Bibliography. Listing the various reasons people might choose to read literature from the past ("amusement or instruction or moral elevation or escape", for "an encounter with transcendence, for visceral engagement with past conflicts, for a glimpse of something alien"), Marcus pointed out that each purpose would need a different form of the text and a different approach to assembling it editorially (1). In her analysis, editions were all relative, dependent upon the aims of the editor and reader, and no perfect text could supply all the needs of all possible ends. Indeed, the more an editor strained towards this pure, ideal text, the more likely it was that they would be influenced by the assumptions of their own time and context. Being vividly aware of the cultural and social influences we operate under, of the influences that have shaped the form texts were transmitted in, and of the continual mediating effect which gets between us and the author, are far safer ways to proceed, in Marcus' view.

> No single version of a literary work . . . can offer us the fond dream of unmediated access to an author or to his or her era; the more aware we are of the processes of mediation to which a given edition has been subject, the less likely we are to be caught up in a constricting hermeneutic knot by which the shaping hand of the editor is mistaken for the intention of the author, or for some lost "perfect" version of the author's creation.
>
> (3)

The call to "unedit" texts, to reverse the mental processes that valorised a pure, ideal text that emerged from the clutter of material processes and historical accidents which had supposedly obscured it, deliberately blurred a line that had previously been drawn between textual scholars and literary critics. The vision of editors and bibliographers as the essential first stage in a process, recovering and fixing the text before handing it on to other scholars who would interpret and analyse it, was a staple of the New Bibliography. They saw their task as establishing the basic data which could then be used by literary critics to build interpretations, and assumed that if a critic failed to use a properly edited text then their reading of the work would be at risk of basic flaws. Literary analysis was an activity that could be carried out once the safe boundaries of the text had been established, marked and reproduced by a definitive edition. As Marcus pointed out, the suspicion that the move towards "unediting" cast upon the single, pure, ideal text undermined the assumption that editing was a task to be undertaken once for all. The interpretations based upon a text might send the scholar back to the editorial processes that produced a particular edition, not to suggest that there had been a single mistake that could be rectified to reinstate that edition as perfect, but (far more threateningly to New Bibliographic ideas) to uncover other entirely valid possibilities that might conflict but could not rule each other out of court.

Marcus provides a powerful example in making her case for the instability of textual meaning, and the need for humility in fixing and glossing meanings. The description of Sycorax as "blew-eyed" in *The Tempest* has been the subject of extensive comment and even emendation, as she demonstrates. Various critics and editors have suggested that it meant having a blue tinge to her eyelids, making the comparison to plays such as *The Duchess of Malfi*, which refer to this as a sign of pregnancy. Others changed the adjective to "blear-eyed", or documented examples of early modern texts which used "blue-eyed" to refer to the dark circles around the eyes signifying illness or tiredness. Still others traced the language used of eyes in both courtly and demotic poetic registers, suggesting that grey eyes were considered most beautiful in the native tradition, and that the blue eyes that appear in poetic *blazon* were an import from Continental literary traditions. All of this scholarly activity has stemmed from one impulse, which is hidden by the very erudition and research that it caused: the need to explain – or explain away – the suggestion that Sycorax had blue eyes. As Marcus points out, this is only a problem in the text if a whole host of cultural baggage is brought with the reader or editor: that blue eyes are beautiful, that white, European (blonde, blue eyed) people provide the standard by which beauty is judged, that people from North Africa cannot quite qualify as beautiful, that the reader will assume that they are on the side of white European people in terms of physical appearance and aesthetic worldview, that Sycorax must be established and maintained as a racial "other" within the play, and so on. The meticulous scholarship that presented early modern beliefs about pregnancy, eye colour, poetic tradition, and the rest, is being marshalled in the service of an essentially colonial view of what constitutes beauty and whose side the audience should be on.

As with her comments about textual history, Marcus' most trenchant critique here does not suggest that the wrong answer has been reached, or that the scholarly work which produced that answer contains serious errors of process, but that the very agenda which launched it must come under scrutiny. It is the question, not the answer, which Marcus' work queries. Particularly in this example, her analysis undermines the New Bibliography's hopes of certainty and a definitive text by underlining the dependence of meaning upon time, interpretation and cultural context. It also chips away at the reliability of consensus judgement between textual scholars by suggesting how that judgement can be conditioned by the training and background of those scholars, to the point where some questions seem absolutely natural and others never arise.

Biblical Studies has also seen a critique of the assumptions underlying much traditional textual criticism, and – like Marcus and the "unediting" movement – it emerged from scholarship that combined a concern with the early forms of the documents with an interest in their history of development and interpretation. In *The Living Text of the Gospels* and *Textual Scholarship and the Making of the New Testament*, David C. Parker has emphasised the scribal processes that gave rise to the manuscripts as we possess them. He stresses the alterations and developments made in this process as part of a Christian tradition of reflection upon faith, rather than a gradual corruption of an original, pure text. For Parker, "manuscripts do not carry a tradition. They *are* that tradition", and he rejects "the idea that there is a greater reality *behind* what we have" (*Living*, 209). Where traditional textual criticism hopes to reconstruct an original text, or even the original sayings that circulated in oral tradition before that text was written down, Parker embraces the historical situatedness of the texts we have. Just as the early church continued to debate and interpret the meaning of its faith, leading to the decisions of the great councils of the fourth century over its understanding of Christ, the scribal tradition was part of an ongoing Christian practice. The written tradition was influenced by a pre-existing oral tradition, which continued alongside and was itself influenced in turn by the written tradition. The Church canonised four Gospels, all of which differ in some points, not because Christians hoped that somehow they contained enough truth to be more or less reliable and could be sieved thoroughly later to produce the facts, but because all were understood to provide a witness to the revelation of God in Jesus. In the latter book, Parker suggests that the books of the New Testament should each be regarded as "a process and not an object" (*Textual*, 21), and that in fact "the modern concept of a single authoritative 'original' text" is "a hopeless anachronism" irrelevant to early Christianity (24). He argues that the activities of reading, copying and commenting upon the central works of Christianity were part of a holistic process, guided by participation in the life of a Christian community and inspired by the Holy Spirit, not separate actions. Parker draws on the Pauline distinction between the "letter" and the "spirit" to offer this as a theological as well as a textual argument (24).

So textual scholarship has produced a complex set of procedures and guidelines for working on texts, as well as a critique of its methods and assumptions. The more attention is focused on the historical conditions that gave rise to modern texts, the more we find we need to reassess the categories that are so often taken for granted, such as "original", "authorial" or "correct" texts. The "unediting" theories in Shakespeare Studies call for a reassessment of the idea of a single correct text, in favour of a variety of editions tailored for different purposes, and a recognition that apparently neutral and objective editing activities are often ideologically coded. The work of David C. Parker argues for the replacement of "text as object" by "text as process", integrating the activities of copying, interpretation and alteration into a living Christian tradition. As became clear in the examination of the canon, scholarly work on the text of Shakespeare and the Bible has provided historical information, as well as showing how modern concepts are themselves part of a particular historical moment. We may need to formulate new questions as well as searching for the answers we thought we wanted.

3.
Ways of Reading

This chapter explores some of the methods of interpretation that are applied to Shakespeare and the Bible. I have called it "ways of reading" to highlight the fact that these approaches to the texts may vary a great deal in their presuppositions, their processes and their results, but they are all carrying out the same task. A reader who picks apart references to women in the New Testament to reveal a story of female leadership half-buried in the text which subsequent Christians tried to erase, and a reader who searches Revelation to determine whether Iran is ushering in the end of the world have radically different agendas. They might be expected to disagree not only on what the Bible says, but on how we should even go about reading it, and what criteria we can use to determine whether our own individual impression is an accurate version of "what the Bible says".

Nonetheless, they are both engaged in a close scrutiny of the text, and their reading techniques may have more in common than first appears. They are both concerned with the details of the text, believing that it is only by close attention to particulars that the true meaning will be made clear. They both approach the texts expecting them to hold a weight of significance that is not obvious on the surface (one of the factors that we saw John Barton ascribing to "sacred texts" in the introduction). They both assume that the texts have something important to say about the world beyond the page, and are not simply aesthetic patterns whose value lies in their formal complexity, or free-floating narratives which can refer only to the world within their own pages. They both believe that this "something important" is part of a powerful current which has run through the entirety of human history, having an impact on a global scale, and which holds a central importance in world events, affecting even those who don't understand it or know it exists. They both apply specialist strategies of reading in order to be alert to the nuances and details that will be important for their interpretation. They both work on the assumption that the most vital meaning of the text is somehow hidden or obscure, and can only be recovered by those who know hidden meanings exist and can search for them patiently.

These forms of interpretation thus share some presuppositions both about the text and about the way in which it needs to be read, even if they also differ drastically in their other presuppositions and in the process they carry out. To people who don't share their broader religious and social ideas – including many readers of this book, no doubt – their reading might look less like a search for meaning and more like the imposition of their own ideas. Yet deliberately applying methods of interpretation (or ways of reading) do seem to have been necessary over the centuries when dealing with these texts. History has demonstrated that people will disagree sincerely, and even violently, over what seems to them to be perfectly evident and obvious in the text. The Reformation's call to attend to the "plain sense" of the Bible, to reshape Christianity around the simple meaning of what was written, detonated a reaction that split Protestantism again and again. The proliferation of Protestant groups in Britain during the sixteenth and seventeenth centuries, from Anabaptists to Fifth-Monarchy Men, from Muggletonians to Calvinists, gives a pessimistic view of the chances for Christians reading the Bible and spontaneously agreeing what it means. Christian Smith has described this as "pervasive interpretative pluralism", a situation in which readers of the Bible have continually failed to find the same meaning within it, and he cites Vincent de Lerins in the fifth century remarking that

> Owing to the depth of Holy Scripture, all do not accept it in one and the same sense, but one understands its words in one way, another in another, so that it seems capable of as many interpretations as there are interpreters.
>
> (Smith, 21)

As Smith points out, even Luther, who had presumed that his own challenge to Roman Catholic doctrine was based upon the evident meaning of the Bible, came to believe that a system of interpretation was needed, since the other groups within the Reformation produced doctrines so different from his own. He commented, with typical acerbity, on their method:

> I learn now that it is enough to throw many passages together helter-skelter, whether they fit or not. If this be the way then I can easily prove from Scripture that beer is better than wine.
>
> (Smith, 21)

Smith himself has examined the variety of doctrines and interpretations that are discussed in one particular version of Christianity (American Evangelical Protestantism), and noted the popular books that present debates between Evangelical scholars, under the title of "Four Views On . . ." topics such as war, women in ministry, baptism and divorce. Having collated all the titles, and computed the number of doctrinal positions they represented, then multiplied them by each other to discover the number of separate combinations of doctrinal opinions they represent, Smith presents his results. The opinions on these issues identified by these books, within a relatively narrow theological spectrum, could result in more than five million different sets of beliefs. Clearly "what the Bible says" varies considerably depending upon the reader. This is most noticeable amongst the groups Smith investigates – Evangelical US Protestants – because of the central place they accord the Bible in their religious practice and view of the world, and the fact that they regard themselves as the heirs of the sixteenth-century Reformers. Contrasting their "Biblical" Christianity with the emphasis laid upon reading the Bible in the light of "tradition" (for more Catholic Christians) and "reason" (within Liberal Christian groups), US Evangelicals centre their religious identity on their reading of the Bible. As Smith has suggested, this reading is not as stable as might be hoped, and has produced a plethora of different opinions, with a resulting galaxy of small denominations as groups split off from their original churches when they came to disagree on the "clear" meaning of Scripture.

Indeed, the Bible itself contains several mentions of perplexity and the difficulty of finding the correct reading. The book of Acts relates the story of Philip meeting an official of the Ethiopian queen, who was busy reading the Scriptures:

> So Philip . . . heard him reading the prophet Isaiah. He asked, "Do you understand what you are reading?" He replied, "How can I, unless someone guides me?"
>
> (Acts 8:30-1)

Differences in the interpretation of Shakespeare have been less dramatic in their effect on the lives of those involved, but they are nonetheless capable of evoking strong disagreement on the meaning of the same text. This does not always stay as a difference of opinion over a particular passage of poetry, and often involves the clashing of opposed views of the world. The radical theatre director Charles Marowitz once commented that he actively disliked having to "share" Shakespeare with those whose political and moral opinions differed from his:

> I have to say, quite frankly, that some of the most contemptible people I have ever known have loved Shakespeare, and I have found that very hard to take. It's like sharing your bed with bigots and junkies. For many of them, Shakespeare is a confirmation of their world view. The Christian Universe is memorialized in his work, and, from his sentiments, they can easily justify their bourgeois smugness, their conventionality, and their pompous morality. For them, it is as if Shakespeare wrote only so that they could quote his aphorisms on their calendars.
>
> (17)

For Marowitz, and for many others, the central place Shakespeare occupies in the cultural canon means that disagreeing about what Shakespeare means is tantamount to disagreeing about how society should be run, about how people should live, about what is natural, about what is worthwhile, and even what constitutes reality. The history of Shakespeare criticism has produced a radical Shakespeare who reveals the contradictions in the military-monarchy complex, a capitalist Shakespeare who encourages the reader to work hard and act prudently, and a feminist Shakespeare who depicts the horrific choices forced on women by an oppressive male society, to pick only a few from a massive spectrum of readings. As with the Bible, there is apparently no chance of simply reading the text and agreeing on what it means, let alone coming to a consensus on how that meaning should affect the way we act.

So interpretation seems a necessity. Robert Morgan and John Barton provide a definition of this term at the opening of their book on *Biblical Interpretation*:

> Interpretation is an intermediary task performed by rational human beings to make human communication possible in difficult cases. In interpreting we first understand the human utterance and then elucidate it for ourselves or someone else.

Whereas mechanical transmitters pass on messages by relaying sounds or transcribing them into a more permanent form, interpreters often say something quite different in order to get across the *meaning* of an utterance. Unlike the proverbial horse and mule, or the products of modern technology (artificial intelligence is a borderline case), interpreters have *understanding*.

(1)

Their definition brings out a number of themes that will be useful to keep in mind as I examine the various methods of interpretations that are used to explore Shakespeare and the Bible. They stress the difficulty involved in cases of interpretation. Simply hearing someone speaking and understanding them does not count as interpretation, even very briefly and easily, for Barton and Morgan. This means that the activity always involves a recognition that "interpretation" comes into play during a snag or a knot in the processes of communication on which we rely in our everyday lives. It also implies that the interpreter should acknowledge the possibility of other solutions to the "difficult case" they are faced with.

In the second part of the definition they deliberately stress the element of paraphrase or explanation involved. Merely repeating the message loudly and clearly does not count as interpretation (despite the valiant efforts in this direction familiar to anyone who has found themselves amongst British tourists abroad). Interpretation might require saying "something quite different" in order for the listener or reader to appreciate the true meaning of the message (or passage of text) that has caused the difficulty. In order to do this, they need to have understood the meaning themselves – or to believe they have – beyond the original form in which it was phrased. In the example I rather unfairly gave about my fellow Brits on holiday, someone who was sent to the bar by a friend to get "Two pints of Foster's" and was met with incomprehension might try "Two beers – large beers – lagers – Australian – Amber Nectar? – same as we had yesterday – two from that blue tap there, please?" But if they did not themselves know what the order meant, though they had memorised the words, they could only continue repeating "Two pints of Foster's" in a state of increasing thirst.

There are resources for students studying Shakespeare that highlight this element of interpretation by printing entire line-by-line paraphrases of Shakespearean plays. For example, Hamlet's most famous soliloquy begins with these lines:

To be, or not to be? That is the question –
Whether 'tis nobler in the mind to suffer
The slings and arrows of outrageous fortune,
Or to take arms against a sea of troubles,
And, by opposing, end them? To die, to sleep –
No more – and by a sleep to say we end
The heartache and the thousand natural shocks
That flesh is heir to – 'tis a consummation
Devoutly to be wished!

(III: i: 58-64)

In the version of the play offered by *No Fear Shakespeare*, this becomes:

> The question is: is it better to be alive or dead? Is it nobler to put up with all the nasty things that luck throws your way, or to fight against all those troubles by simply putting an end to them once and for all? Dying, sleeping – that's all dying is – a sleep that ends all the heartache and shocks that life on earth gives us – that's an achievement to wish for.

This is where interpretation becomes more obviously contentious, since interpreting the text involves a claim to have understood it (and perhaps an implication that the interpreter has understood it better than those to whom they are speaking). English teachers might object that "luck" is not an exact equivalent of "fortune" in Hamlet's words, and the aside "no more" has a richer resonance in a speech about death than can be explained by "that's all dying is". They might object that this paraphrase is reductionist, and thins down Shakespeare's meanings into an easily-digestible form that misses the complexity and poetic nuance of the original. This accusation can be levelled against all interpretation that explains difficult words by substituting others in their place, from the simplest notes in the margin to explain unfamiliar vocabulary, to the most abstruse and contentious theological interpretation. The more involved the interpretation becomes, and the more words are involved in elucidating the original text, the more likely it is that the interpreter will be accused of over-reading, of finding meanings that were not present in the text when they came to it. As this chapter will show, there is no neutral or objective ground from which such judgements can be made. Everyone involved in interpretation believes that they are accurately and effectively reproducing the real meanings of the text, and suspects others of importing irrelevant or unsuitable material connected to their own agenda and worldview.

In this chapter, I will be examining a series of ways of reading. I will not be able to offer a complete survey of the ways Shakespeare and the Bible have been read and interpreted; even if I had space to do so, there are other scholars who have already provided in-depth and thorough accounts. Instead I will be juxtaposing and contrasting radically different approaches to how these texts should be read, comparing character criticism with stage-centred criticism, and placing allegory next to literal readings. As elsewhere in this book, I will provide various quotations from earlier authors, in order to show not only what they thought but the ways in which they expressed it. (This will also give readers the opportunity to disagree with my interpretations and paraphrases of the passages I have quoted.) I will not cover the schools of critical theory that have become such an influence on contemporary readings of these texts, such as Marxism, feminism and structuralism. This is not because I think these critical frameworks are unimportant or trivial (on the contrary, I find feminist scholarship probably the most productive way of reading both texts in modern culture). It is simply because these critical approaches would take the chapter beyond its scope as a sampling of the modes in which the texts have been read, and into an examination of the ideological agendas those readings support and serve. Mode and ideology cannot be entirely separated, as will become clear below, but I have attempted to keep the focus on the processes involved in reading, within the space available.

The Bible and Allegory (Two-Fold, Four-Fold and Manifold)

The interpretation of the Bible found a focus in two major traditions in the ancient world, which became attached to the names of Antioch and Alexandria.[1] The Antiochene school stressed the more literal and historical meaning of the text, whilst the Alexandrian school, whose most famous exponent was Origen, was much more engaged with allegorical and symbolic readings. The Christian works of the Alexandrian interpreters were influenced by Philo, a Jewish scholar who employed allegory to explain the Hebrew Scriptures in the light

---

1. A clear and concise account of various tendencies in the history of Biblical interpretation is provided by David Grant and Robert Tracey in *A Short History of the Interpretation of the Bible*, as quoted in this chapter.

of Greek philosophy. Thus for Philo the image of the seven-branched candelabrum, so strongly present in rabbinic Judaism, represents the seven planets of the universe, and in the narratives of the patriarchs, Abraham and Sara represent the ethical values of Mind and Virtue (Grant and Tracy, 53). This approach was developed in a specifically Christian way by Clement and Origen, whose work searched the Scriptures for hidden connections and spiritual implications. Not only did they find philosophical and ethical meanings in the texts revered by Christians, but they found Christian meanings in the narratives and prophecies of the Hebrew Scriptures. In Origen's work, this developed into a theory about the connection of history and Scripture with the ultimate meaning of things, as revealed through Christ:

> Because the principal aim was to announce the connection that exists between spiritual events, those that have already happened and those that are yet to come to pass, whenever the Word [or Christ] found that things which had happened in history could be harmonized with these mystical events he used them, concealing from the multitude their deeper meaning.
>
> (cited in Grant and Tracey, 57)

The real interest for Origen and the Alexandrians was not the truths of history but the larger spiritual implications that were spelled out in hidden and mystical ways through historical events. Indeed, Origen used this to account for the fact that the Scriptures did not always seem to relate the literal truth:

> But wherever in the narrative the accomplishment of some particular deeds, which had been previously recorded for the sake of their more mystical meanings, did not correspond with the sequence of the intellectual truths, the scripture wove into the story something which did not happen, occasionally something which could not happen, and occasionally something which might have happened but in fact did not.
>
> (cited in Grant and Tracy, 57)

Here Origen takes the allegorical and mystical method (and the theory explaining it) so far that the world itself seems to become rather irrelevant. It can sometimes be used to explain the deeper "intellectual truths" that must be communicated, but sometimes it is not even capable of that. Given this attitude to the universe and the "real" spiritual world beyond it, Origen's thought has a lot in common with the Gnostics discussed in a previous chapter, who rigidly separated the material and spiritual worlds and believed that religion was a way of escaping the debased sphere of the physical.

Medieval interpretation in the Western church developed various "senses", or types of meaning that could be sought in the Scriptures. Though there were various systems and accounts of how these senses worked, the most famous summing up is the "four-fold exegesis", or four-part interpretation, which appears in the work of Thomas Aquinas. These senses, or ways a text can mean something, are as follows:

- the literal sense, or the historical or factual meaning to which the passage refers;
- the allegorical, which expresses under symbolic or cryptic images certain religious truths;
- the moral, which provides ethical instruction about how one should live and relate to others now;
- and the anagogical, which refers forward to heavenly or eschatological matters after the end of this world as we know it.[1]

These may seem very abstruse, so it is worth focusing on a particular example that demonstrates the way in which they can all apply in various ways (and perhaps at various times) to the same term, drawing on the monastic writer John Cassian's discussion of the significance of "Jerusalem" in the Bible, and relating the senses to meanings and associations which a modern reader could find in the word. Cassian states that

> One and the same Jerusalem can be taken in four senses: historically as the city of the Jews, allegorically as the Church of Christ, anagogically as the heavenly city of God . . . tropologically as the soul of man, which is frequently subject to praise and blame from the Lord under this title.
>
> (cited in van Liere, 122)

These categories can also sit within a contemporary Christian reading of the image. In the literal sense, Jerusalem is a historical location, the capital city of the Jewish people, in which the Temple was located and to which people made journeys at certain religious festivals. It was threatened, besieged, captured and destroyed at various points, as referred to in the documents of Christianity and other sources.

---

1. Frans van Liere gives an absorbing and readable account of medieval exegesis and its various aspects in *An Introduction to the Medieval Bible*.

In the moral sense, Jerusalem is an image of the human soul, a city surrounded by dangers and subject to praise and blame by God. It contains the capacity for human life to fully flourish and to develop all the potential for arts, culture and sociability that clustered around cities in the ancient world (and which are still present in cities today, so long as the Wi-Fi doesn't cut out). However, it is also subject to being taken over by destructive impulses, by the tendencies towards harm and vice every human personality also contains, and which can overpower the positive aspects or even twist them towards a negative purpose.

In the allegorical sense, Jerusalem is the Church of Christ, the holy city recreated and renewed in the community of believers. The access to holiness and transcendence represented by the Temple within Jerusalem are understood as available to all who follow Christ. Their identity is centred upon something that took place in Jerusalem: the crucifixion and resurrection of the Incarnate God, who was condemned there and sent out of the city to be killed, but appeared miraculously amongst his followers as they mourned him, and whose spirit descended upon them at Pentecost in Jerusalem forty days later. Every day, all over the world, a ritual meal is held by members of this body to remember or re-enact a meal which took place in that city.

Finally, in the anagogical sense, Jerusalem is the heavenly city, the focus of Christian hope and longing for a world that will be remade at the end of human time, resembling this world in ways which will reveal the most profound and transcendent truths that have been immanent in the world we have experienced, but which have only been glimpsed obscurely and confusedly. The work of redemption and salvation that was visible at various points in Jerusalem – from its seat as the royal house of David to the arrival of a Messiah in the city who was understood as the rightful descendant of David – will be completed in the new Jerusalem, described by religious poets as a shining city.

These various meanings could seem rather strained or tenuous when simply listed like that, or assigned one by one to a mention of Jerusalem in a Biblical passage. However, we can recognise a plethora of "senses" in which Jerusalem is used in literature and politics beyond the medieval exegesis of the Bible. It stands as a potent political and national symbol for many people in the Middle East and simply using the name embroils their discourse in such a powerful system of symbols and principles. As I was writing this book, the US Supreme Court heard the case known as *Zivotofsky v. Kerry*, which technically ruled on a point of law over the President's control over foreign affairs, but which was sparked by a family who wanted their son's passport to specify that being born in Jerusalem meant he had been born in Israel. At the same time, a serious and heated debate was being carried on in Britain about the welfare state, particularly the National Health Service. These institutions were created in the late 1940s, under Britain's first majority Labour government, who explicitly set out to create a socialist "New Jerusalem" for the nation. Somewhat further back in history, Augustine of Hippo used the image of Jerusalem in his *City of God*, in the aftermath of the sack of Rome, to sketch a trajectory of history in which the triumph of Christ did not depend upon the success of the Roman Empire. In the face of the apparent defeat of a Christian empire, Augustine looked to a heavenly city in which the hopes of the people of God would be fulfilled. (Though it originates in a phrase from the Sermon on the Mount, it is probable that the longevity of the image of a "city on a hill", which has resounded through American politics ever since John Winthrop used it in a sermon in the 1630s, owes something to the holy city of Jesus' own time.)

These scattered instances suggest that we are still attuned to symbolic and metaphorical resonances clustering around a term that is apparently literal and descriptive, even if not all modern readers find the four-fold exegesis a comfortable way to read. Indeed, given the wide range of the meanings I have just outlined, it is significant that part of the function of the exegetical structure was to constrain interpretation as well as expand its possibilities. A single term might be assigned four meanings – where a casual or literal reader might register only one – but those meanings are part of an explicitly Christian reading of the text. The luxuriance of the range of meanings released by the medieval exegetes is paralleled by an insistence that this is a Christian book that should be explored in a particular spiritual and religious direction.

Literal Reading (and Being Literally Wrong)

The most obvious contrast to an allegorical method of reading is the literal, which focuses attention upon the surface meaning of the text rather than seeking a symbolic or hidden meaning. Ancient interpretation had included a literal tendency, which was associated with Antioch just as the allegorical strain of thought was more connected with Alexandria. The reading methods that emerged during the European Reformation often emphasised the literal sense as a way to liberate the text from the over-determined and obscure results of medieval exegesis. An outright critique of the medieval system of interpretation is given in William Tyndale's *Obedience of a Christian Man*, a classic of the English Reformation:

> They divide the scripture into four senses, the literal, tropological, allegorical and anagogical. The literal sense is become nothing at all. For the Pope hath taken it clean away and hath made it his possession. He hath partly locked it up with the false and counterfeited keys of his traditions, ceremonies, and feigned lies, and partly driveth me from it with violence of the sword.
>
> (in King, 41)

He goes on to object to the method by which the four-fold exegesis separates out the meanings, but the main thrust of his objection is clear here: such sophisticated systems of reading obscure the plain and simple meaning of the text. The message of a Biblical passage, according to Tyndale, is swallowed up in an elaborate set of "traditions" and "feigned lies", ensuring that no-one who reads the Bible can see how it challenges Roman Catholic doctrine and practice. The system determines the meanings that can come out of the Bible in advance, channelling everything the text appears to say in pre-approved directions. The effect is not entirely seamless, however, as he emphasises the way that the Pope has to apply coercion to keep everyone agreeing with the official interpretation "with violence of the sword". Tyndale instructs his reader not to be bamboozled by these ways of reading:

> Thou shalt understand therefore that the scripture hath but one sense which is the literal sense. And that literal sense is the root and ground of all and the anchor that never faileth where unto if thou cleave, thou canst never err or go out of the way. And if thou leave the literal sense, thou canst not but go out of the way.
>
> (in King, 41)

Tyndale's language here is saturated with Biblical imagery: even as he makes an argument about the best way to interpret the Bible, he positions himself and his antagonists within the narratives that the volume contains. The Pope keeps the real meaning of the Scriptures locked up with "false and counterfeited keys", which disputes the Roman church's claim that the Pope has inherited from St. Peter the "keys" to salvation given in Jesus' declaration that "I will give you the keys of the kingdom of heaven" (Matthew 16:19). The literal sense is obscured by the "traditions" of Roman Catholic interpretation, echoing Jesus' criticisms of the "traditions" that the Pharisees impose upon the Scriptures (in passages such as Matthew 15), and a true reader cannot leave "the way", which Jesus declared himself to be in John 14:6: "I am the way, the truth and the life, and no-one comes to the Father except by me". Thus, though Tyndale argues for a literal and plain approach, he still values the images and metaphors that his own writing appropriates from the Bible.

Literal interpretation of the Bible has often been associated with very conservative, even fundamentalist, forms of Christianity. Radical right-wing Christians in the US and UK are often assumed to be people who "take the Bible literally", and they certainly accuse those from different traditions of not doing so. However, as James Barr has pointed out in his book *Fundamentalism*, such groups more often interpret the Bible both literally and non-literally at different times, in order to confirm their own attitudes to the Bible intact. A concern for the Bible's absolute verbal inerrancy and lack of error on any point, for example, leads some to suggest that the "six days" in which Genesis declares that the world was created are in fact representative of six geological ages, six moments spaced widely apart in history, or six days which happened after a long period of preliminary development (Barr, 41-3). The literal meaning of the verses are clear, and the book of Genesis elsewhere shows a great concern for genealogy, time and the precise specifying of events, but many fundamentalists allow this passage to have a "symbolic" or non-literal meaning in order to preserve the idea of the Bible as entirely without any historical or geographical error. Other passages may be taken literally, in that efforts are taken to explain events in a way that guarantees that what is written in the Bible took place in history, but in a way which drains them of their significance within the story. For example, the stories of the manna in the wilderness or the crossing of the Red Sea have been subjected to elaborate explanation by particularly conservative interpreters, with reference to the peculiar meteorological and environmental conditions of the area (see Barr, 241-2). This saves the Bible from presenting stories that cannot be believed because they are impossible, and allows the fundamentalist readership to continue to credit the Bible with utter accuracy in every single

detail of its narratives. However, it does so at the expense of the
meaning of the event within the narrative: the manna and the
Red Sea are described as mighty and miraculous acts of God, not
extremely unexpected but useful combinations of circumstance. A
"literal" interpretation is made, in the sense that the words in the
Bible are assumed to have a specific reference to an actual physical
event in the world, but their broader meaning according to the
book is distorted.

Indeed, it can be suggested that a literal reading of the Bible is
the only basis upon which truly sceptical and critical work may be
carried out. A straightforward reading, attending only to the literal
meaning and discounting theological or other explanations, can be
alert to discrepancies and problems that are ignored by a devotional
reading. As Barr suggests, "if one passage gives . . . a mere three
generations from Levi to Moses, while another puts the period at
430 years", or if one version of the story of Hagar describes her
child as a baby and another as a youth of about seventeen, "it might
be considered possible that there were two different sources" which
preserved "different traditions about the same set of historical
relations" (46-7). Where one Gospel places the cleansing of the
Temple at the beginning of Jesus' ministry, and another at the end,
a literal reading is forced to deal with the apparent discrepancy. The
entire apparatus of historical-critical research depends upon taking
the text literally, because only if it is taken literally – rather than
taken in whatever sense preserves the inerrancy of the Bible – can
the documents be recognised in their different outlines.

This is not to say that taking the text literally disproves the
truth of the Bible or renders it insignificant: historical-critical
readings are generally concerned with understanding the origins
and meaning of the Biblical documents, not spotting "errors" that
disprove "inerrancy". In Barr's phrase, it is possible to say that
"the critical approach to biblical literature is the one in which it
becomes . . . possible to understand the literature without having to
use the category of 'error'" (55). For the historical-critical scholar,
the text says what it says, and explanations must be sought for that
meaning, but this does not constitute hunting for "errors", because
the fundamentalist attitude towards the Bible's meaning is not
assumed in the first place. The literal way of reading is therefore
not as closely aligned with a very conservative religious attitude as is
often assumed.

The Bible and Behind the Bible

A "historical" mode of reading could cover several ways of approaching and using the text, all of which treat the Biblical books as historical documents, but which follow different procedures and aim at different results. It is possible to read the Biblical books as historical evidence, considering them as sources that give information about the events and people to which they refer. This can range from a fundamentalist insistence on the literal days of creation and the historicity of the narratives about Moses, to a more nuanced use of the text to inform our understanding of Jewish history. Secondly, a "historical" reading might be one that set the Biblical books within their historical context, as far as we know it. This could involve understanding the diet and sanitary laws within Leviticus in terms of their place in a nomadic society's practical demands and overall worldview. It might involve investigating the system by which Roman rule was carried out by client states in the Middle East during the first century, in order to understand better the disproportionate part that taxes and tax collectors might seem to play in the religious controversies surrounding Jesus' ministry. Thirdly, a historical approach could attempt to read beyond and behind the Biblical books, seeing them as interventions in the historical record, which possess their own agenda and which must be interrogated and questioned. This kind of reading would ask why these narratives were preserved, whose interests they served, and what version of history they are trying to validate.

In Biblical criticism, a "historical" reading often means employing the collection of tools and strategies brought together under the label of "the historical-critical method". The precise limits and basis of this method are disputed – as indeed is the question of whether it is a method at all – but it involves a set of related reading practices and scholarly approaches that have some assumptions in common. They focus on the sorts of historical readings I outlined above; they are interested in the world that the text refers to, which shaped the text's development, as well as the history of the text itself. On finding a contradiction or a problem within the text, an allegorical reading might use it to point to a deeper "spiritual" meaning, whereas a historical reading might call into question the literal accuracy of the text, and investigate its development or its historical setting. It is often suggested that fundamentalist Christians read the Bible "literally", when they espouse Creationism or suggest that the Second Coming will take place before long. However, as James Barr has argued at some length, historical critics deserve the adjective "literal" far more often. If one part of the story of Hagar suggests her son was fourteen when she fled into the desert, and another part states that she carried him on her shoulder like a baby, many conservative interpreters will seek to reconcile these apparently contradictory details. When Jesus seems to get a quotation from the Old Testament wrong, or Paul's account of a disagreement within the church does not tally with another account in the New Testament, there are plenty of readers ready to explain away these sticking points.

The historical critic sees no such problem: for them the text is to be read literally. It says what it says. If that means the texts contradict each other, or seem to have internal problems, that is not a particular worry for the historical-critical approach. It investigates the text's literal meaning, even if that comes at the expense of its authority. We might say that a literal reading – a reading that simply identifies (as far as possible) what the text says and doesn't mind if that's awkward – is the necessary first step for a historical-critical approach.

Sayings (and Who Can Say)

A good example of one particular kind of historical reading is provided by the ways in which Biblical scholars scrutinise the words and actions of Jesus as reported in the Gospels. In trying to analyse the Gospel materials, a collection of criteria have been developed in order to produce a coherent and probable account of the events and speeches that lie behind the texts we now possess. Scholars "test" particular sayings or stories by comparing them with these criteria. It's worth pointing out that this is not an entirely rigid methodology, but a set of principles that can be invoked to classify and discuss sayings and events. Rather like the principles of textual criticism, they are articulations of critical ideas that need to be deployed and managed by scholars who use them to build and test critical judgements.

The criterion of embarrassment is perhaps the most memorably-named of the principles. It states that material which is troubling or inconvenient for the overall picture of Jesus presented by the Bible is more likely than not to be authentic. Thus the baptism of Jesus by John, which seems to imply that Jesus might have been one of John's followers, regarded him as his religious master, or accepted his authority in some sense, fulfils the criterion of embarrassment.

Behind this principle is the idea that it guards to some extent against the rewriting of traditions or later interpolation of material. Christian communities would be unlikely to invent stories about Jesus and the Apostles that cast them in an awkward or unimpressive light.

Connected to this is the criterion of discontinuity, the principle that a saying or teaching that does not accord with the doctrines or practices of Christianity at the time when the Gospel was being collected and circulated is more likely to be considered authentic. This rests on a similar assumption to the criterion of embarrassment: that people would be unlikely to spontaneously create teachings, and ascribe them to Jesus, which contradicted their own religious ethos. Such material is more likely to have been grudgingly remembered and transmitted *despite* its awkward status.

The criterion of "multiple attestation" is a more complex formulation of a relatively simple idea: that a particular passage or feature is more likely to be authentic if it appears in independent sources. This operates at the level of texts and at the level of genre. Thus a feature is strengthened if it appears in different Gospels, whilst not apparently being part of one Gospel's influence on another. This is a fairly common-sense point about the balance of evidence, familiar from our own media literacy which makes us tend to trust information or opinions that come from many news outlets which are independent from each other, and similar to the journalistic practice of confirming a sensational report by seeking other sources that back it up. Multiple attestation in genre is the assumption that a particular motif or image is more significant if it appears in different kinds of discourse, such as parable, prophecy, or ethical teaching. A useful example of this is given by John P. Meier, when he points out that the "Kingdom of God" occurs across both different sources and different forms. If we had it only in a parable, or in prophetic material, we might imagine it was a vivid image coined for entirely literary or dramatic purposes, rather than a consistent and substantial part of Jesus' religious teaching.

The criterion of coherence is also a straightforward principle: that once we have a fairly large corpus of material which seems to be authentic, passages and sayings can be tested against the general collection to see if they make sense alongside it. Once the general outlines of a picture of Jesus' life and teachings have emerged, scholars have the opportunity to test the coherence of material under question. The final criterion is less an individual principle, and more a reminder or warning: the criterion of Jesus' rejection and execution. This is a test applied to the whole image and account of Jesus produced by scholarship, rather than a way of holding up individual motifs or quotations for scrutiny. It reminds scholars that Jesus was arrested, tortured and executed by the authorities, and asks them if the image they have produced of him can make sense within this framework. Meier paints this challenge posed to certain academic reconstructions of Jesus with broad strokes:

> While I do not agree with those who turn Jesus into a violent revolutionary or political agitator, scholars who favour a revolutionary Jesus do have a point. A tweedy poetaster who spent his time spinning out parables and Japanese koans, a literary aesthete who toyed with 1st-century deconstructionism, or a bland Jesus who simply told people to look at the lilies of the field – such a Jesus would threaten no one, just as the university professors who create him threaten no one.
>
> (in Dunn and McKnight, 136)

As I mentioned above, these criteria are tools designed to be used by a community of scholars to debate and test their hypotheses, rather than straightforward methodological rules that can be followed mechanically to produce a result. There are potential flaws in all of them, if applied too simply or to an extreme. The criterion of embarrassment, if it was used to determine all decisions, would produce an image of Jesus made up only of negative or confusing elements, a religious leader who could not have inspired his followers either before or after his death. The criterion of discontinuity, if overused, would tend towards a Jesus who had no connection with the worship and ideas of either the Judaism from which he emerged, or the Christianity that revered him later. Any actions or sayings that made sense within those systems would be highly suspect, leaving us only with a detached, abstract figure who could not be connected with much human life. There is also a distinct risk that in the absence of an emphasis on Jesus' Jewishness, troubling strains in Christian thought would reassert themselves: too much reflection on his life and ministry has sought to detach him from the Jewish people and his own Judaism.

The criterion of coherence could encourage us towards smoothing out anything striking or paradoxical in Jesus' teachings, anything that went beyond either a rigid scheme of images and their explanations or a general moralising emphasis on being nice to people. It would also find itself at striking variance with the discontinuous and baffling Jesus being produced by the first two criteria. The criterion of multiple attestation could unintentionally overlook vital elements in the sources because they only happened to be recorded by one document, and combine with the criterion of coherence in its quest for a Jesus of the lowest common moral denominator. Finally, the criterion of rejection and execution would valorise a Jesus who could barely speak to anyone without trying to overturn their tables or telling them to go back to the nest of vipers where they were born, leading us to wonder how he might have gained the following he did. All of these are caricatures, of course, but they highlight the caricaturing effect of over-emphasising particular criteria, or using them as rules instead of guiding principles. On a broader level, the criteria need to be wielded carefully because they are specifically set up to deal with the material we possess about Jesus and the problems and challenges it poses. They are not historiographical principles which would work equally well to produce a biography of Albert Einstein, or to sift the theories about Alexander the Great's personal opinions. They have emerged out of the history of Biblical scholarship, and so they have been shaped by the aims and assumptions of that project. They perhaps work best as concise articulations of certain principles and certain risks that scholars should bear in mind when exercising their own judgement.

Shakespeare: Character, Theme and Family Size

Shakespeare's works have given rise to a range of reading strategies, equally specific to their history of interpretation. One mode, character criticism, is an approach that probably seems natural to many modern readers. It takes the plays to be narratives in which striking and intriguing people take the centre of the stage, whose actions, personalities and motives hold our attention. Character criticism encourages us to regard the fictional characters rather as we would people in the world beyond the play: to like them, or despise them, or wonder why they do what they do. It allows us to imagine that they have a rounded, psychologically complex existence, one that we often imagine stretches far beyond the events and conversations we actually see portrayed on stage. Many people will have encountered this kind of critical approach at school, with exercises such as rewriting a scene as an entry in one character's diary, being asked to suggest what happens next after the end of the play, or to imagine how a character would act if they were transported to the present day. It's also a major part of the way actors workshop and prepare for a performance. One popular exercise involves putting one actor in a "hot seat" for two minutes whilst the other members of the theatre group ask them questions and they have to respond in character. It allows (or forces) the performer to develop their sense of the hinterland of personality and experience that lies beyond the character's actions and words in the script. Actors will sometimes say that in order to inhabit a character on stage, they need to invent details such as where that character sleeps, what their favourite food is, what they're afraid of, who they want to be. Working in this way involves assuming – even if the scholar, school student and actor all know this is a pretence – that the character has some form of existence beyond the words on the page.

In academic Shakespeare criticism, one of the major works that follows this approach is A.C. Bradley's *Shakespearean Tragedy*. The book's subtitle – *Lectures on Hamlet, Othello, King Lear, Macbeth* – already hints at the way in which Bradley sees the defining elements of Shakespeare's tragic plays, choosing as the paradigmatic examples plays whose titles are the names of individual men. For Bradley, understanding Shakespeare's great tragedies involves tracing the motives and actions of the heroes. Fate, chance, plot and poetry are all involved as well, but mainly as they impinge on the central figure who provides the fascination and the lynchpin for the work. At one point he suggests how differently we would read *Hamlet* without the unusual and complex hero:

> Suppose you were to describe the plot of *Hamlet* to a person quite ignorant of the play, and suppose you were careful to tell your hearer nothing about Hamlet's character. Would he not exclaim: "What a sensational story! Why, here are some eight violent deaths, not to speak of adultery, a ghost, a mad woman and a fight in a grave! If I did not know that the play was Shakespeare's, I should have thought it must have been one of those early tragedies of blood and horror from which he is said to have redeemed the stage"? And would he not then go on to ask: "But why in the world did not Hamlet obey the Ghost at once, and so save seven of those eight lives?"

(89)

Bradley concludes from this imagined anecdote that "This exclamation and this question both show the same thing, that the whole story turns upon the peculiar character of the hero" (89).

His analysis of the play is close and thorough, working through the motives and feelings of Hamlet himself, and the same treatment is given to Othello, Macbeth and King Lear. The notes which Bradley adds to this discussion of the hero give a flavour of his attitude to the play: these include "Events before the opening of the action in *Hamlet*", "Where was Hamlet at the time of his father's death?" and a discussion of "Hamlet's age", amongst other matters. These are excellent examples of the way in which character criticism treats the plays as small histories, whose characters existed before the curtain was raised and whose stories extend either side of the wings. To a formalist or a Marxist critic, the question of "Where was Hamlet at the time of his father's death?" might be answered briefly by saying that Hamlet was off-stage and therefore didn't exist at the time, with a note that Hamlet's father only ever appears as a ghost, so his death isn't part of the narrative that *Hamlet* relates. Though Bradley clearly knows that Hamlet was not a real person, for him the most productive way to analyse the play is to focus in on the hero and treat him as a psychologically-rounded personality, with his own intentions, feelings and internal conflicts.

This form of character criticism is not one of the main ways in which academic criticism has studied Shakespeare since the mid-twentieth century, though it is still noticeable in school classrooms and actors' workshops, as I mentioned above. The novelistic, psychological attitude it encourages towards the plays was condemned in an article by L. C. Knights, entitled "How Many Children Had Lady Macbeth?" The title is somewhat misleading, since Knights does not enquire into the family situation of Macbeth's wife, but criticises Bradley and the character-centred criticism for irrelevant pedantry. Calling his essay "How Many Children Had Lady Macbeth?" is Knights' way of mocking the approach that produced Bradley's note on "Hamlet's age" and "Events before the opening of the action in *Hamlet*". He sets out his critical stance early in this essay, declaring that when it comes to current Shakespeare criticism:

> the most fruitful of irrelevancies is the assumption that Shakespeare was pre-eminently a great "creator of characters". So extensive was his knowledge of the human heart (so runs the popular opinion) that he was able to project himself into the minds of an infinite variety of men and women and present them "real as life" before us. Of course, he was a great poet as well, but the poetry is an added grace which gives to

the atmosphere of the plays a touch of "magic" and which provides us with the thrill of single memorable lines and lyric passages.

(1)

By way of demonstration, he refers to recent lectures by the actress Ellen Terry, which focused on the life of the characters, including her discussion of how a minor character in *Henry V* came to speak a foreign language: "Robin's French is quite fluent. Did he learn to speak the lingo from Prince Hal, or from Falstaff in London, or did he pick it up during his few weeks in France with the army?" (2). Amidst all the popular and academic treatment of Shakespeare, Knights states, there is no recognition of the fact that "character" is just an illusion produced by the words of the play; like "plot" or "rhythm" it is an abstract idea that is created in the audience's mind. The characters have no real existence, only the words do: a Shakespeare play is a "dramatic poem" in which the humans are as much symbols as the imaginary landscape in which the action takes place or the images of a poetic speech. Knights advises that this approach can provide valuable insights into the hero-centred plays covered by Bradley, such as *Macbeth, Othello, King Lear* and *Hamlet*, and that "it is the only approach which will enable us to say anything at all relevant about plays like *Measure for Measure* or *Troilus and Cressida* which have consistently baffled the critics". Looking for the central hero with a set of psychological conflicts and an extensive backstory is certainly unlikely to make sense of either of those plays.

When Knights comes to explain his own method of thinking about the plays, he frames them in terms of theme, not character. *Macbeth* is not a study of a rounded, complex personality for him, but "a statement of evil".

> Two main themes, which can only be separated for the purpose of analysis, are blended in the play – the themes of the reversal of values and of unnatural disorder. And closely related to each is a third theme, that of the deceitful appearance, and consequent doubt, uncertainty and confusion. . . . Each theme is stated in the first act. The first scene, every word of which will bear the closest scrutiny, strikes one dominant chord

(18)

This is clearly a very different way of treating the plays to drawing up timetables of the plot, or speculating on where the main characters were educated and how they felt about their childhood. Knights' essay proved a turning point in the general direction of academic study, and character criticism has been largely out of fashion during the twentieth century. There have been some revivals of interest in "character", however, in the early twenty-first century, including the sweeping theories of Harold Bloom's best-seller *Shakespeare: The Invention of the Human* and the more rigorous and theoretical work of Jessica Slights and Paul Yachnin. Modern uses of "character" in academic criticism tend to focus less on the idea that there are "people" within the plays who can be investigated, and more on the way in which audiences and readers interact with the fictional figures as if they were people during the process of interpretation.

Images, Patterns and Spaniels

Where Bradley found fascinating characters, and Knights discussed abstract themes, other critics have approached Shakespeare as a poet whose work can be best understood through formal qualities. Since the plays are densely-wrought works in verse, they seek to tease out the significance of poetic elements, from rhythm and rhyme to systems of imagery. This approach is most famously associated with the "New Criticism" of the twentieth century, which scorned the biographical and impressionistic critical strains it saw in the nineteenth century and encouraged a focus on the formal aspects of literature. If character criticism treated the plays as if they were nineteenth-century novels, the paradigmatic literary form for New Criticism was the lyric poem: short, self-contained, highly patterned and capable of being read and understood on its own terms. Along with this stress on the formal qualities of a poem came a concern with its coherence and organic unity, both of which appeal to the work itself as the defining source of its own meaning and significance. This is not to say that New Criticism preferred its literature straightforward and simple. Quite the reverse was true: the exponents of this mode valued irony, ambiguity and nuance, poetic qualities that appeared all the more impressive when they were produced by the verbal patterns of a poem itself. The title of Cleanth Brooks' collection of essays *The Well-Wrought Urn* provides a powerful image of poetry viewed from a New Critical perspective: the literary work standing as an artefact, possibly discovered long after its creator was dead, embodying a source of aesthetic wonder and a store of meanings. This title suggests poetry is not an act of communication, or a game played together by people following intricate rules, but a made object, an almost physical thing in the world. The image is part of New Criticism's rejection of historicist or biographical readings of literature, which tied the value of works to the situations in which they were created and received, and denied the possibility of transhistorical judgements, or the possibility of literary works being valued for their inherent quality regardless of context and origin. Enmeshed with this critical philosophy was a certain critical practice: close reading. For many people who have passed through the British or US educational systems, taking a discrete passage of literary material and analysing its qualities and features often seems a natural and self-evident way to understand texts. If you are used to facing a page's worth of poetry on an examination paper, armed with nothing but your wits and what you can remember of the way iambic pentameter is supposed to sound, this can look like the default mode of reading. It does encode particular assumptions about literature, however. Carrying out "practical criticism" (as it is also known) on a previously unseen poem involves a belief that its meaning will not be dependent on the situation in which it was composed, or the originally intended audience, or the author's biography (though all these may influence it). It encourages a focus on the technical aspects of the literary text: metre, rhyme, rhythm, patterns of imagery, references that are generally recognisable (such as Biblical or classical references), rhetorical techniques and tropes. The poem is implicitly framed as a more closed system, with its potential meanings encoded within itself.

The turn towards studying image systems, though it did depend on a close scrutiny of the text, could still be combined with a concern to understand Shakespeare's mind and personality, rather than dividing the author from the text. Caroline Spurgeon's 1936 book *Shakespeare's Imagery and What It Tells Us* examines particular networks of images, and relates them to events in Shakespeare's life or tendencies in his thought. One of the most remarkable is her tracing of the connections between imagery around dogs, sweets and false friendship. She explains at the beginning of her discussion of these images that

> It is quite certain that one of the things which rouses Shakespeare's bitterest and deepest indignation is feigned love and affection assumed for a selfish end. He who values so intensely – above all else in human life – devoted and

disinterested love, turns almost sick when he watches flatterers and sycophants bowing and cringing to the rich and powerful purely in order to get something out of them for themselves.

(195)

The tenses here show a blurring between Shakespeare the person and Shakespeare the text, as discussed in the earlier chapter on textual criticism. The text that is immediately available to the reader is combined with the personality of the author and his personal feelings, so it is in the present that Shakespeare's indignation is roused and his feelings expressed. Spurgeon moves from the emotions displayed in the text to the events and experiences which she surmises had caused them.

> It is as certain as anything can be, short of direct proof, that he had been hurt, directly or indirectly, in this particular way. No one who reads his words carefully can doubt that he had either watched someone, whose friendship he prized, being deceived by fawning flatterers, or that he himself had suffered from a false friend or friends who, for their own ends, had drawn out his love while remaining "themselves as stone".

(195)

In elaborating her position, Spurgeon refers to a whole sequence of passages in which flattery or the expression of false friendship appears, noting that they share a set of images:

> Now whenever the idea, which affects him emotionally, of false friends or flatterers occurs, we find a rather curious set of images which play round it. These are: a dog or spaniel, fawning and licking; candy, sugar or sweets, thawing or melting. So strong is the association of these ideas in Shakespeare's mind that it does not matter which of these items he starts with – dog or sugar or melting – it almost invariably, when used in this application, gives rise to the whole series.

(195)

To demonstrate her claim, she cites extensively: Metellus Cimber's rebuke from Caesar for thinking that Caesar would be "thaw'd" with "that which melteth fools, I mean, sweet words/Low-crooked court'sies and base spaniel-fawning"; Hamlet's reference to "the candied tongue" that licks "absurd pomp . . . where thrift may follow fawning"; Hotspur's exclamation at "what a candy deal of courtesy/

This fawning greyhound then did proffer me"; Antony's scorn for "the hearts/That spaniel'd me at heel" which now "do discandy, melt their sweets/On blossoming Caesar" and for "Villains" for "fawn'd like hounds . . . kissing Caesar's feet" whilst "Casca, like a cur, behind/ Struck Caesar on the neck. O, you flatterers!" (196).

Having established the curious verbal pattern, after explaining her impression of Shakespeare's emotional and moral inner life, she then historicises the image system by presenting a hypothesis as to why these ideas might be connected. It's important to note that the opinion about Shakespeare's moral sentiment is not *reached* by the network of words Spurgeon is elaborating, but precedes it. Careful attention to his words reveals this particular aspect of Shakespeare's writing, from which a deduction is made about his personality, and then the image system – which in itself does not prove he was hurt by a false friend, and is not introduced to do so – is revealed and discussed. In fact, Spurgeon's conclusion in this section of *Shakespeare's Imagery* involves trying to explain why these apparently unconnected concepts are clustered in his work (and therefore his mind):

> The explanation of this curious and repeated sequence of ideas is, I think, very simple. It was the habit in Elizabethan times to have dogs, which were chiefly of the spaniel and greyhound type, at table, licking the hands of the guests, fawning and begging for sweetmeats with which they were fed, and of which, if they were like dogs today, they ate too many, dropping them in a semi-melting condition all over the place. Shakespeare, who was unusually fastidious, hated the habit, as he disliked all dirt and messiness, especially connected with food.
>
> (197)

She goes on to explain that "there come to be linked in his mind two things he intensely dislikes", the "fawning cupboard love of dogs, their greed and gluttony, with its sticky and disagreeable consequences" in the physical world, and in the emotional world "the fawning of insincere friends, bowing and flattering for what they hope to get, and turning their back when they think no more is coming to them" (197). The combination of certain emotional scars in Shakespeare's life, and certain physical conditions under which life was lived in his period, have fused together phrases that do not seem to belong together when read four hundred years later. The question implicitly posed by Spurgeon's title is answered: Shakespeare's imagery tells us something about his emotional life and his personal habits.

Staged Readings and Reading the Stage

All the approaches to Shakespeare I have discussed so far can be criticised for treating the plays as if they were another kind of writing, whether novel, diary or lyric poem. Performance criticism, or stage-centred criticism, developed most fully in the late twentieth century, and prided itself on treating the works as what they were: plays. The beginnings of stage-centred criticism are often traced to the work of William Poel and the Elizabethan Stage Society at the end of the nineteenth century. Poel had become convinced that the major theatres of his time had misunderstood Shakespeare, so to understand his ideas we need to appreciate the way the plays had previously been treated.

The managers of the big theatres in Victorian London mounted big, impressively detailed productions of Shakespeare, with elaborate scenery and large numbers of extras. They strived for an illusionistic effect, in which the audience looked at the stage and saw an entirely convincing fictional world (even if it happened to involve fairies and historical kings). It was no coincidence that the proscenium arch – the huge decorated arch that stretched around the opening of the stage like a picture frame – came into its own during this era. Managers arranged the scenery, actors and movement to produce striking and engrossing stage pictures, like the dramatic historical paintings that dominated the fine arts of the time. Perhaps the most notorious example of this illusionistic style was the set for Herbert Beerbohm Tree's production of *A Midsummer Night's Dream*, for which he imported actual tree trunks with which to build the onstage forest, and set loose live rabbits to frolic around the set and add verisimilitude.

The effects must have been remarkable, but they were also rather ponderous. All the carefully-posed pictures and massive scenery meant that the action had to be arranged around big set-pieces, which could have their impact upon the audience and make the most of all the stage setting. This did not really suit the way the plays had been written, Poel noticed, as Shakespeare's scenes tend to switch in quick succession. Generally speaking, characters move fluidly on and off the stage, and the location can change rapidly from one place to another. That could not be achieved with the bulky Victorian stage sets, and so the plays were chopped up and rearranged to minimise the changes of scene. Even so, when the curtain fell between scenes, it could take ten or twenty minutes of rumbling and banging before it rose again on a new location. Poel and some others felt this rather held up the flow of Shakespeare's narratives, damaged the intricacy of his dramatic construction, and encouraged a bombastic over-heroic style from actors trying to get maximum value out of ponderous set-pieces.

At root, Poel and the Elizabethan Stage Society's criticism of the mainstream theatre of the time was concerned with authenticity. The big theatres had been trying for a certain kind of authenticity with their large illusionistic sets, attempting to depict the settings of the plays in a dramatic and absorbing way. For *Julius Caesar* the architecture of Ancient Rome would be recreated so far as was possible, for *The Merchant of Venice* strenuous attempts would be made to draw the audience into the canals and pageants of Venice, and the history plays were often staged with careful historical research into the correct armour and heraldry for the characters to wear. However, there was another sort of authenticity which this approach ignored: the plays' coherence in themselves, and their relationship to the theatre they were written in. Poel and the Society insisted that Shakespeare had known what he was doing when he wrote the plays, and had crafted them deliberately as pieces of theatre. Taking these works apart to rearrange them into striking and historically accurate stage pictures, in their view, missed the point of them. They were not just a set of brilliant and poetic moments, strung together for a sixteenth-century theatre that unfortunately did not have the resources and scenery of the Victorians; they were deftly-constructed dramatic art designed to fit perfectly within the theatre of the time. In order to recover the true Shakespeare, Poel and the Society attempted to reconstruct the theatrical context he had worked within, or at least to produce a modern approximation of it.

This meant studying the conventions of Shakespeare's theatre as positive parts of the dramatic language and theatrical resources that were available to him as an artist, rather than regarding them as primitive and unfortunate precursors of the Victorian stage. They experimented by producing Shakespeare with limited props, and minimal scenery, speaking the lines in a quicker and more lively style. They were particularly guided by the speech from *Hamlet* in which Hamlet instructs the actors how to perform the play at court:

> Speak the speech, I pray you, as I pronounced it to you, trippingly on the tongue: but if you mouth it, as many of your players do, I had as lief the town-crier spoke my lines.

> Nor do not saw the air too much with your hand, thus, but use all gently; for in the very torrent, tempest, and, as I may say, the whirlwind of passion, you must acquire and beget a temperance that may give it smoothness. O, it offends me to the soul to hear a robustious periwig-pated fellow tear a passion to tatters, to very rags, to split the ears of the groundlings, who for the most part are capable of nothing but inexplicable dumbshows and noise
>
> (III: ii: 1-12)

To the members of the Elizabethan Stage Society, this sounded strikingly like a denunciation of the sort of productions they were criticising, coming from within the Shakespeare canon itself. Their scorn for noise and bombast, and their emphasis on intelligent speaking and listening, seemed to be validated by Shakespeare himself. In their experiments, the words became the central focus instead of the spectacle. They recovered a sense of the plays as an imaginative effort between the audience and the actors, who all entered into a tacit agreement to produce a fictional world from the poetic imagery instead of the visible scenery. It was no longer a problem when scenes switched quickly between Venice and Belmont, or between Italy and Britain. The rapid changes of location built tension and suggested parallels between different strands of the action (rather as cutting between different scenes does in film). The insights that their work produced were influential on a number of later directors, such as Harley Granville-Barker and Peter Hall, and are now part of the mainstream of Shakespeare scholarship, most notably developed in the work of J.L. Styan. Shakespeare's Globe in London is perhaps the most obvious result of Poel's revolt against big-stage illusionistic Shakespeare: an approximate reconstruction of the theatre for which Shakespeare wrote, which has been extraordinarily successful both in informing scholarship and attracting large numbers of theatregoers. The impact of the stage-centred approach is also visible in the majority of large Shakespeare productions: it is no longer unusual to have a mostly bare stage, with scenery chosen for its symbolic value rather than its realistic appearance, and a few telling props, instead of an entire fictional world arranged on the other side of a giant picture frame.

This approach to Shakespeare might sound as if it belongs more to the history of the theatre than to interpretation, but stage-centred criticism insists that only by understanding Shakespeare's plays as theatrical works can we understand them on their own terms. This is both a set of ideas and a way of working: the theatre practitioners and academics who use this approach believe that the stage can also work as a research tool itself. Theories can be tested onstage in a similar way to scientific hypotheses being tested in a laboratory. Obviously the experiments are less precise, and the results cannot be measured with the same kind of exactness, but they see the theatre as the crucible from which real knowledge and understanding of Shakespeare can emerge. There are certainly moments at which meanings emerge in performance that would remain invisible or irrelevant if the text was only studied on the page. The end of *Measure for Measure* is an excellent example. Isabella, a novice nun who was being blackmailed for sex by the Duke's second-in-command Angelo, is saved by the appearance of the Duke himself. The Duke then metes out justice and reward to the virtuous characters in the following speech, addressing the characters on the stage in turn:

> She, Claudio, that you wrong'd, look you restore.
> Joy to you, Mariana! Love her, Angelo:
> I have confess'd her and I know her virtue.
> Thanks, good friend Escalus, for thy much goodness:
> There's more behind that is more gratulate.
> Thanks, provost, for thy care and secrecy:
> We shill employ thee in a worthier place.
> Forgive him, Angelo, that brought you home
> The head of Ragozine for Claudio's:
> The offence pardons itself. Dear Isabel,
> I have a motion much imports your good;
> Whereto if you'll a willing ear incline,
> What's mine is yours and what is yours is mine.
> So, bring us to our palace; where we'll show
> What's yet behind, that's meet you all should know.
>
> (V: i: 439-553)

On the page this brings the play to an end, with the Duke declaring that he intends to marry Isabella, or at least to propose to her, instead of sending her back to the nunnery to take her vows. This poses a problem for some readers, as Isabella has not suggested at any point in the play that she would like to find a husband, and has in fact been the subject of male sexual aggression. The apparently unilateral bestowing of a marriage on a novice nun is a somewhat odd way to wrap up the loose ends here, and critics have disagreed over how "happy" an ending this would have seemed to Shakespeare and his audiences. Whilst this can remain a problem on the page, on stage it has to be solved somehow. Isabella has to be standing on the stage within earshot of the Duke, since he speaks directly to her, but she is given no lines at all. In production the director and actor have to fill the blank space the script provides with some sort of decision: is Isabella delighted, flattered, appalled, defiant, shocked, numb? Even if the actor decides to stand on the stage with an entirely neutral expression, this will have an effect on the meaning of the moment (studiedly neutral expressions not being a traditional way of responding to proposals of marriage). In performance Isabella's reaction – or lack of it – contributes enormously to the meaning of these last lines, and thus the arc of the entire play. Is this a story of injured innocence under threat and then saved, a coming-of-age tale about a young woman whose sexual awakening happens just at the moment when she was about to become a nun, or a dystopic parable about two male tyrants who both want to control women sexually? In practice, the play has been tackled in many ways. On stage the silent Isabella becomes central to the audience's understanding of what has just been shown to them, in a crucial moment that only becomes visible in performance.

Readings, Re-Readings and Counter-Readings

Each of the methods of interpretation I have described has its advantages, and each can provide insights that the others will miss. Character criticism can help an actor to explore and inhabit a fictional role on stage, in order to produce a powerful and convincing performance for the audience. Historical criticism can pose questions about the motives and conditions of the text's production that shed light on gaps and silences in the text itself. Allegorical interpretation can weave a profound and engrossing web of significance within and between Biblical texts, allowing the reader to meditate upon the shape and implications of their religious faith. Performance criticism can bring the plays to life, revealing problems, rhythms and moments of crisis that are invisible whilst the script remains on the page. These methods can also be subject to criticism, either because they provide only a partial perspective or because they can distort the meaning of the books. Character criticism (as we saw above) can be accused of disappearing into a fantasy world where fictional characters have lives as real as ours, not to mention childhoods, family squabbles and preferences in breakfast foods. The five-fold exegesis can be suspected of spreading a veil of obfuscation over what the text actually says, substituting abstruse traditions of interpretation for the literal words and ensuring that no meaning can emerge from the Bible that might challenge the religious system which claims to revere it. Historical criticism might be regarded as taking apart the records of a radical spiritual revival in order to determine trivial details of the material conditions under which it took place, whilst in the process discounting the religious dimension of the events which caused anyone to bother recording them in the first place.

These approaches also make claims about the best way to interpret the texts that are not always reconcilable with each other. It is no coincidence that the accounts I have given above often begin with a disagreement or the proponent of one critical method objecting to another. Differences in approach during interpretation can reveal profound differences in assumptions about what the text is and what it should be used for. At the same time, methods do not determine results: it is possible to use a particular interpretative strategy to produce widely varying conclusions, and to use extremely different reading methods in the service of the same agenda. The feminist critic I imagined at the opening of this chapter could use a historical approach to investigate the institutions and social conditions that lie behind the Biblical text, seeking to reveal a history of women's participation in religion which the extant documents mostly obscure. Or she could reread major episodes in the Bible, such as the Creation narrative, to show that their networks of images and poetry do not necessarily support the subjugation of women, but can be read in the service of their liberation.

Her counterpart in Shakespeare Studies could spend her time attending performances and noting how modern actors release the subversive potential within the plays to call into question gender norms, or she could write accounts of the heroines' characters that called attention to their shaping by a misogynistic society. Much feminist work shifts between these different modes in the pursuit of a specific set of critical and political imperatives. Thus the modes of reading I have sampled above are involved in debates about the relative truth of particular attitudes to the texts, and to the world around them, but can be used in dramatically different ways. In the next chapter I shall take this attention to modes of reading a step further, and examine how the physical activities of reading – from reading out loud in church to silent meditation – involve similar engagement with ideas about the texts' value and interpretation.

4.

Performing the Word

In this chapter I will examine the idea of reading in a more practical sense, concentrating on the ways in which Shakespeare and the Bible are read and how these express assumptions about their meaning. Elsewhere in this book, "reading" means interpretation, making references, quotation and other ways of handling the texts, but this chapter is concerned with how we pronounce the words. How we read matters, whether we speak the words aloud in public to an audience, whisper them to ourselves privately, chant them with a group of other people, or scan them silently with our eyes. Each of these allows different things to happen, encouraging certain meanings to emerge from the text and obscuring others. Central to these issues of reading is the idea of performance, a term that has positive and negative connotations. Both the works of Shakespeare and the Bible contain warnings against the falseness and deceit that can be involved in performance:

> And when you pray, do not be like the hypocrites, for they love to stand and pray at the synagogues and at the street corners, so that they may be seen by others. Truly I tell you, they have received their reward. But whenever you go to pray, go into your room and shut the door and pray to your Father who is in secret; and your Father who sees in secret will reward you. When you are praying, do not heap up empty phrases as the Gentiles do; for they think that they will be heard because of their many words. Do not be like them, for your Father knows what you need before you ask him.
>
> (Matthew 6:5-15)

Seems, madam! nay it is; I know not "seems."
'Tis not alone my inky cloak, good mother,
Nor customary suits of solemn black,

Nor windy suspiration of forced breath,
No, nor the fruitful river in the eye,
Nor the dejected 'havior of the visage,
Together with all forms, moods, shapes of grief,
That can denote me truly: these indeed seem,
For they are actions that a man might play:
But I have that within which passeth show;
These but the trappings and the suits of woe.
                              (*Hamlet*, I: ii: 76-86)

These passages demonstrate a suspicion that still clings to the word "performance" as we use it in general conversation. Jesus' instructions as to how his disciples should pray involve a stern and specific condemnation of the "hypocrites", who make elaborate gestures and expressions in public, as well as the "heathen", who carry out repetitive verbal formulae. He contrasts these with the private and straightforward prayers suitable for addressing God. In the second quotation, Hamlet turns angrily on his mother after she suggests he seems unhappy, picking up on her word "seems" and insisting that his clothes and behaviour cannot explain to her what he actually feels. His emotions go beyond what can be shown by crying, sighing or wearing black clothes. Both passages show scepticism about "performance" in a broad sense of the word, suggesting that the outward actions and appearances of a person do not accurately and effectively represent their inner reality. This may be – as in the case of the hypocrites – because they deliberately put on a show of piety and holiness that God can see they do not possess, or it may be – as with Hamlet – because those inner feelings are so powerful that no outward expression can communicate them meaningfully. Truth is inward, and the authenticity of performance is cast into doubt. Anyone claiming to show truth by their outward actions and gestures should be regarded with suspicion.

However, both texts also include more positive depictions of performance. The end of the Gospel of John (in the NIV wording) relates how "Jesus performed many other signs in the presence of his disciples, which are not recorded in this book". The outward action and in the inward meaning are far more comfortably aligned in this phrasing, and Jesus' signs can be "performed" without either losing or distorting their meaning. *Hamlet* also contains an effective performance, when the prince directs the travelling players to perform a show that will mimic Claudius' supposed murder of

Hamlet's father, and thus cause Claudius to betray himself by his reaction. "The play's the thing, wherein I'll catch the conscience of the king", as Hamlet puts it, and the plan works. Thus performance is also shown as powerful, meaningful, and capable of uniting inner significance and outer actions. In this chapter, I'll explore the performance of the Bible and the works of Shakespeare in public, how it contrasts with private reading, and how people's attitudes to it have varied over the centuries. This will involve a complaint by a nineteenth-century literary critic that someone had put a statue up in Westminster Cathedral, a Puritan preacher furiously condemning the damage done to society by theatres, and the Bishop of Lyons worrying that if people breathe at the wrong moment in a Bible reading they might commit blasphemy. As that brief summary suggests, reading and performance have often been the subjects of anxiety or condemnation in the history of these books, and a lot of the sources I'll be drawing on have a distinctly tetchy tone. This is perhaps unsurprising, as the process of reading and performing involves transmitting the meaning within the text accurately into the world outside it, and the stakes are high for people who care deeply about those meanings. What might be more surprising to modern readers are the particular worries people in the past had about how to read these books, and what they thought might endanger that process. I'll start in the history of Shakespeare, with critics who demonstrated a suspicion of performance, and explore why it seemed unreasonable to them to entrust the playwright's works to the theatre, then move to parallel suspicions around the performance of the Bible before investigating early Christian writers who showed a preference for the performance of Biblical texts.

Shakespeare and the Dangers of Acting

Most school and university courses stress the dramatic quality of Shakespeare's plays, suggesting they were intended for performance and are therefore best understood as works for the theatre. Students are often encouraged to get to grips with the plays by reading out speeches, or acting out particular scenes, on the assumption that these texts make most sense when they are put into action. This seems entirely logical, given the plays' origin within the theatrical scene of early modern London, and the way they have been transmitted, as I discussed in the chapters on canonicity and textual criticism. However, this has not always been the dominant view of

Shakespeare's plays. The current focus on the author as a man of the theatre, and his plays as documents of performance, developed during the twentieth century, following an interest sparked by some late nineteenth-century scholars and performers in the original conditions of Shakespeare's theatre. To previous generations it was much less clear that Shakespeare's plays were naturally at home in the theatre. Indeed, as we will see, some went as far as denying that it was possible to properly stage them at all, and argued that reading the plays – rather than acting them – was the only way to truly appreciate Shakespeare's art.

This strain of thought developed through the eighteenth and nineteenth centuries, as Shakespeare came to be regarded as a major icon of literary and national culture, rather than simply as another talented writer. Alongside the elevation of Shakespeare's genius came a focus on the experience of reading (rather than watching) his works. In the preface to his edition of the plays, Samuel Johnson suggests that reading can encompass everything of serious value that a stage production would produce, declaring that a "play read, affects the mind like a play acted" and that a "dramatick exhibition is a book recited with concomitants that encrease or diminish its effect" (28). He does not deny that stage acting can add to the audience's enjoyment of comedy, with gestures and "grimace[s]", but states that "imperial tragedy" is always more impressive and powerful on the page. Johnson takes the view that whatever is most valuable about Shakespeare's works can be experienced through reading, and whatever will be improved by theatrical performance is inevitably more frivolous. He argues that this is a mark of civilisation and maturity, claiming that "as knowledge advances, pleasure passes from the eye to the ear, but returns, as it declines, from the ear to the eye", even seeming vaguely surprised "that we still find that on our stage something must be done as well as said".

Samuel Taylor Coleridge continued the strand of appreciation that Johnson's remarks demonstrate. Coleridge described Shakespeare in the early nineteenth century using somewhat elaborate terms:

> Clothed in radiant armour, and authorized by titles sure and manifold, as a poet, Shakespeare came forward to demand the throne of fame, as the dramatic poet of England. His excellences compelled even his contemporaries to seat him on that throne, although there were other giants in those days contending for the same honour. Hereafter I would fain endeavour to make

out the title of the English drama as created by, and existing in, Shakespeare, and its right to the supremacy of dramatic excellence in general.

(218)

However, despite this praise of his dramatic abilities, Coleridge also insisted:

But he had shown himself a poet, previously to his appearance as a dramatic poet; and had no *Lear*, no *Othello*, no *Henry IV.*, no *Twelfth Night* ever appeared, we must have admitted that Shakespeare possessed the chief, if not every, requisite of a poet – deep feeling and exquisite sense of beauty, both as exhibited to the eye in the combinations of form, and to the ear in sweet and appropriate melody . . .

(218)

The passage goes on to enumerate the various qualities that Coleridge believes are necessary to a poet, but it is striking that he insists Shakespeare possessed these, and had given evidence of them, before he ever wrote for the theatre. Coleridge appreciates the plays, but appears to want to "save" Shakespeare from the stage, asserting that his qualities as a poet are not inherently tied to the medium.

The most dramatic and memorable – not to say extreme – articulation of this idea came in Charles Lamb's essay "On the Tragedies of Shakspere Considered with Reference to Their Fitness for Stage Representation". Lamb criticised the high praise that was lavished on actors who appeared in Shakespeare's roles, declaring that the set of skills which could produce a literary masterpiece had little in common with those which merely represented characters on the stage. He demanded:

what connection that absolute mastery over the heart and soul of man, which a great dramatic poet possesses, has with those low tricks upon the eye and ear, which a player by observing a few general effects, which some common passion, as grief, anger, etc., usually has upon the gestures and exterior . . .

(46)

An author had to understand the internal life of people's minds, Lamb argued, appreciating the origin and nature of their thoughts and feelings, whereas an actor just had to carry out "the bare imitation of the signs of these passions in the countenance or gesture" (46). Tellingly, he complains that an actor's performance is not capable of showing the "motives and the grounds of the passion" in ways that distinguish the feeling "from the same passion in low and vulgar natures" (46). For him, there is great pleasure to be had from watching Shakespeare performed, but it is the same pleasure that can be achieved from any decent and popular playwright. The genius and the insight that make Shakespeare distinct are entirely lost, in his account: "instead of realising an idea, we have only materialised and brought down a fine vision to the standard of flesh and blood" (47). This stress on the ideal and the imagination, the "free conceptions" that are "cramped and pressed down to the measure of a strait-lacing actuality", comes out strongly in his complaint that *Hamlet* becomes vulgar and crude if performed because an actor has to keep his mind on the effect he is producing on every member of the audience, whereas the true Hamlet was "shy, negligent, retiring" (47, 49).

> Why, nine parts in ten of what Hamlet does, are transactions between himself and his moral sense, they are the effusions of his solitary musings, which he retires to holes and corners and the most sequestered parts of the palace to *pour* forth; or rather, they are the silent meditations with which his bosom is bursting, reduced to words for the sake of the reader, who must else remain ignorant of what is passing there. These profound sorrows, these light-and-noise-abhorring ruminations, which the tongue scarce dares utter to deaf walls and chambers, how can they be represented by a gesticulating actor, who comes and mouths them out before an audience, making four hundred people his confidants at once?
>
> (48-9)

In this extraordinary passage, Lamb seems to imply that the necessity for words in literary art might itself be a bit regrettable. The conceptualisation of character in the author's mind seems to be the definitive act of artistic creation for Lamb, and the communication of that character undergoes one form of diffusion by the text's words, and a second by the performance of a play's text on the stage. It is an oddly Platonic idea, which echoes Plato's scorn for artists since everything in the world was a copy of its ideal form, and therefore mimetic art could only offer copies of copies. Lamb claims that "I am not arguing that *Hamlet* should not be acted, but how much *Hamlet* is made another thing by being acted" (49). He has no such scruples about *King Lear*, however: "the Lear of Shakespeare cannot be acted" (55).

> The greatness of Lear is not in corporal dimension, but in intellectual: the explosions of his passion are terrible as a volcano: they are storms turning up and disclosing to the bottom that sea his mind, with all its vast riches. It is his mind which is laid bare. This case of flesh and blood seems too insignificant to be thought on; even as he himself neglects it. On the stage we see nothing but corporal infirmities and weakness, the impotence of rage; while we read it, we see not Lear, but we are Lear – we are in his mind, we are sustained by a grandeur which baffles the malice of daughters and storms; in the aberrations of his reason, we discover a mighty irregular power of reasoning, immethodised from the ordinary purposes of life, but exerting its powers, as the wind blows where it listeth, at will upon the corruptions and abuses of mankind.
>
> (55-6)

Seeing *Lear* performed, "to see an old man tottering about the stage with a walking-stick, turned out of doors by his daughters in a rainy night", is described as "painful and disgusting" (55). Lamb is adamant: "Lear is essentially impossible to be represented on a stage" (56).

Though Lamb expresses his critical strictures with a great deal of style, and obviously has an enormous appreciation for what he considers to be Shakespeare's essential qualities, a lot of modern readers will be surprised at the idea that some of the playwright's greatest works should never be allowed near a theatre. So what can account for an opinion that seems so illogical and perverse to us now? Whilst it's not possible to be absolutely definite about cause and effect, it is fair to say that this focus on reading Shakespeare is bound up in the history of the theatre and the history of reading in British culture. The public theatres of Shakespeare's day, though immensely popular, were not socially elite spaces. They were designed for public entertainment, and must have been noisy, smelly and crowded. In the same space as the actors being paid for theatrical performances there would have been other people selling other kinds of pleasure, including food, drink and sex. The business model of theatres involved the casual transgression of social and sexual boundaries which were carefully policed elsewhere in Elizabethan society: different social classes mixed with each other, young men dressed up as women for the enjoyment of the spectators, and socially-negligible actors impersonated their social betters.

The charges which Lamb levels at actors – that they are common, vulgar, incompetent and pander to people's simplest pleasures – are mild compared to some of the denunciations of the theatres printed in the late sixteenth century. Stephen Gosson's *Plays Confuted in Five Acts* was published in 1582, and denounced the terrible moral example that plays set in front of their audiences:

> The argument of tragedies is wrath, cruelty, incest, injury, murder whether violent by sword or voluntary by poison; the persons, gods, goddesses, furies, fiends, kings, queens, and mighty men. The ground work of comedies is love, cozenage, flattery, bawdry, sly conveyance of whoredom; the persons, cooks, queans, knaves, parasites, courtesans, lecherous old men, amorous young men.
>
> (cited in Pollard, 94)

Beyond the plots of particular plays (of which he clearly disapproved), Gosson argues that the very act of theatrical performance is wrong:

> The proof is evident, the consequent is necessary, that in stage plays for a boy to put on the attire, the gesture, the passions of a woman; for a mean person to take upon him the title of a prince, with counterfeit port and train; is by outwards signs to show themselves otherwise than as they are, and so within the compass of a lie . . .
>
> (in Pollard, 102)

Another critic of the theatre, Phillip Stubbes, complained that theatres "draw people from hearing the word of God, from godly lectures and sermons" and, "these goodly pageants being done", encouraged audiences to satisfy the emotional and physical appetites the drama had roused: "in their secret conclaves (covertly) they play the sodomites, or worse" (in Pollard, 120-1). Alongside these lavish rhetorical denunciations on moral and religious grounds, contemporary critics of early modern theatre suggested that plays encouraged apprentices to neglect their work and that they were philosophically unsound. This last charge was buttressed by reference to Plato's banishing of poets from his ideal city in *The Republic*, on the grounds that since the physical world is an imitation of the real ideal world, artists can only produce an imitation of an imitation. Lamb's comments, which I quote above, clearly have something in common with these earlier critiques of the theatrical scene where Shakespeare's plays originated. Whilst he does not go as far as condemning all artists (quite the reverse), he has taken on some of the Platonic objections to imitations of imitations. He also displays a parallel anxiety about the potential for theatre to blur social distinctions and break down hierarchies. In Gosson this is a blurring of God-given gender and social roles via acting, with socially-dubious men impersonating women and nobles, but in Lamb it is more focused around the way both acting and watching plays mixes up fine and discriminating minds with "low" and "vulgar" people.

Thus Lamb's writing betrays a sense that acting operates at a lower level than reading in several modes; it is philosophically lower, aesthetically lower and socially lower. Indeed, part of the fervour of his critique may come from his suspicions that acting was no longer staying in its place, and might threaten to overtake reading. The first passage of "On the Tragedies of Shakspere Considered with Reference to Their Fitness for Stage Representation" opens with Lamb remarking that he had been walking in Westminster Abbey and noticed a statue of the famous Shakespearean actor David Garrick, next to a plaque with a poem that suggested Garrick and Shakespeare were equal in talent. Lamb was "not a little scandalized at the introduction of theatrical airs and gestures into a place set apart to remind us of the saddest [most serious] realities", and the essay moves from what he obviously considers an impertinence to more general reflections on acting and Shakespeare. It is worth noting that the statue was not entirely unexpected or out of place: Lamb was not just complaining that someone had inexplicably left an actor's image in a church. The statue (which is still there) occupies a niche in the part of Westminster Abbey known as "Poets' Corner", where the graves and monuments of famous writers were set up. The custom originated with Geoffrey Chaucer and Edmund Spenser, and was well established by the time Garrick's memorial statue was erected in 1779. Ten years before his death, the actor had staged a Grand Jubilee in Stratford-upon-Avon to celebrate Shakespeare's life, which had become a phenomenon in the national newspapers, and served to bolster both the rising status of Shakespeare as the national poet and Garrick's identification with the playwright and his legacy. Garrick himself marked the highest point of the acting profession's respectability to date, and paved the way for the later generations of actors who mixed with high society, sent their children to the same school as the gentry, and were received at court. About a hundred years after Garrick's death, Henry Irving would become the first knighted British actor and end his career with honorary doctorates and an invitation to give lectures at Cambridge.

As we have seen, Lamb's criticisms are part of a longer tradition of anti-theatrical suspicion, and sit within a tradition that runs back through Coleridge, Johnson and the Puritan preachers of the sixteenth century. They do not stem solely from his irritation at the pretentious language applied to Garrick's talents. However, it is telling that his essay takes as its pretext the presence of the actor's statue in a corner of the national cathedral that had been reserved for poets. Shakespeare's own memorial had only appeared there in 1740, as he became established as a central figure of British national identity and culture. To Lamb's horror, a mere actor was being installed as the authoritative interpreter of Shakespeare, and his morally and philosophically trivial activities were being regarded as the correct way to approach the great truths that lay within Shakespeare's works. Perhaps his horror at the idea of acting Shakespeare on the stage seems ridiculous to us, but we can recognise in our own times the same strains of anti-theatrical and anti-performance thought. We might disagree vigorously with Lamb's opinions, but they are a useful way to shed light on the history of Shakespeare's image. They might also encourage us to question why our attitudes to Shakespeare and the theatre seem so obvious and natural, given that they were not shared by many of the major literary figures of the past who also claimed to appreciate and venerate his works.

The Bible and a Suspicion of Sitting Quietly

The suspicion of performance – and specifically theatrical performance – that we saw in the previous section is even more visible when we turn from the history of Shakespearean theatre to the history of the Bible. The word "theatrical" itself, as it exists in modern English, contains an implied value judgement, built up over years of usage. More than just meaning "of the theatre", it implies flashiness, insincerity, a gap between reality and appearance. The *Oxford English Dictionary* provides a damning range of synonyms in its account of the word's range of meaning: extravagantly or irrelevantly histrionic; "artificial, affected, assumed . . . 'stagy'; calculated for display, showy, spectacular". The *OED* cites usages of the word at various points to demonstrate its meaning in context, and several of them are intriguing given the subject of this chapter: "To dispense God's Word . . . in poor destitute Parishes . . . more meet for my decayed Voice . . . than in Theatrical and great Audience" (1558); "Turning their . . . services and ceremonies into theatricals" (1706); "If Charles had not carried his love of theatricals to church" (1849). These are only examples from the dictionary, but it is noticeable that religious language reappears in such widely spaced examples, implicitly being used to define the negative connotations of "theatrical".

A recent work on Scripture from the conservative side of American Evangelicalism employs the same combination of ideas to discuss the public reading of the Bible in worship. Edited by Wayne Grudem, C. John Collins and Thomas R. Schreiner, *Understanding Scripture* contains a chapter entitled "Reading the Bible for Preaching and Public Worship", in which R. Kent Hughes advises that public reading "can also prove ineffective if the reading itself is left to a last-minute assignment, such that the reader fails to prepare mentally and spiritually for what he or she is required to do". That failure can lead to be the Bible being "abused by a reader who hasn't the faintest idea of the meaning of what he is reading, or by reading too fast, or mispronouncing common words, or by losing the place". However, in warning against these errors, Hughes is wary of his readers falling into another trap: "[t]his is not to suggest that the Scripture is to be read as dramatically as possible or performed as a reader's theater". This is, strikingly, the only time Hughes uses the word "perform" in his account of public reading and preaching, and he does not specify what "a reader's theater" would involve. He assumes his audience are well aware of the negative connotations of "theater", and can appreciate without further explanation why it is totally unsuitable for the reading of the Bible. He suggests that, as preparation for reading a particular passage in public worship, "[p]astors and readers can serve their congregations well by prayerfully reading the text a dozen times with pencil in hand *before* reading it to God's people".

Failure in public reading, for Hughes, is located in two kinds of erroneous performance. Firstly, there are readers who perform ineffectively: they read at the wrong pace, or cannot pronounce the names properly, or mix up the passage they are reading from. These are all mistakes in translating the words on the page into public speech, misfires in the smooth operation of turning alphabetical symbols into sounds that the audience understand. Secondly, there are readers who perform too much, who put on an affected or overwrought performance, so that the text's meaning becomes strained or subdued under the personality of the performer. Despite these all being problems with performance, Hughes does not present practical solutions around the technique of public reading in order to stave off such problems. He does not, for example, advise taking a series of deep breaths before reading, or practising projecting the voice so that it can be heard in a large room without the reader having to put overpowering emphasis on particular words. His solution is to read the text multiple times, "with pencil in hand", essentially sending the reader back to the page to solve problems of performance. He assumes that if any reader has understood the meaning of the text as it exists on the page, then the translation into public performance will be seamless and natural. In this account of reading the Bible in worship, performance is only ever a problem, not a solution. We can tell that the activity has gone wrong if performance (or even "theater") seems to be taking place, and the way to solve that is not by better performance (or techniques borrowed from the theatre), but by more studious private reading.

That might feel like a rather elaborate reading of a few casual sentences in a work that is, after all, designed to be helpful to the general Christian reader rather than to develop a theory of performance. It might seem unfair to Hughes to scrutinise his comments so closely and examine the assumptions behind them. However, the casual nature of his remarks is the very reason that I think it is worth paying attention to what he wrote. As is evident throughout this book, so much of what we believe about both Shakespeare and the Bible is not explicitly stated but encoded into the assumptions and practices that surround our handling of them. The most radical and profound philosophical principles we hold about these books are those which we never even notice, because they seem so self-evident. Hughes is of interest precisely because performance appears so fleetingly and uncomfortably in his account of worship and preaching. There are other writers, who show similar attitudes in much more dramatic ways (if that adjective is not too unfortunate a pun). When complaining about the "ritualist" High Church services held at St. Alban's Holborn in nineteenth-century London, Lord Shaftesbury drew on theatrical language to utterly condemn them:

> In outward form and ritual, it is the worship of Jupiter and
> Juno . . . such a scene of theatrical gymnastics, and singing,
> screaming, genuflections, such strange movements of the
> priests, their backs almost always to the people, as I never
> saw before even in a Romish temple. . . . The communicants
> went up to the tune of soft music, as though it had been a
> melodrama, and one was astonished, at the close, that there
> was no fall of the curtain.
>
> (in Chapman, Chapter 4)

As with Hughes, it is worth noticing the details of this passage,
though they are slightly drowned out by the vehemence of
Shaftesbury's disapproval. Two ideas are blended together and
opposed to the way a service should be conducted: classical pagan
cults and the theatre. The former, with its reference to "the worship
of Jupiter and Juno", combines a suggestion that this form of
church ritual has so deviated from the proper way of worshipping
as to be essentially non-Christian, with a suggested elision of the
gap between Roman classical deities and Roman Catholicism,
picked up in the mention of a "Romish temple". The (by now
familiar) contrast between the gravitas of Christian religion and
the frivolity of the theatre is used to discredit the worship at St.
Alban's by recasting the distinctive aspects of the liturgy (such as
chanting, bowing and processing) in terms more appropriate to
entertainment: "theatrical gymnastics", "soft music, as though it
had been a melodrama", "fall of the curtain".

Scrutinising these terms further, we might notice that Shaftesbury
compares the service to particular kinds of theatrical performance:
melodrama and gymnastics were regarded by Victorians as
"illegitimate" genres, in contrast to the "legitimate" forms of
high tragedy and polite comedy, exemplified by Shakespeare. The
distinction, created by the Patent Act in 1737, which restricted
the production of "legitimate" drama to certain royally-licensed
theatres, had technically been abolished by the Theatres Regulation
Act of 1843, but continued to dominate Victorian attitudes to
stage performance. Shaftesbury is – whether deliberately or not
– describing the ritualist service in terms of the cheapest and
most despised forms of drama, frequented by the working classes
and tellingly called "illegitimate". Another detail might escape
us on casual reading, since the furious Earl does not mention it
explicitly: he is complaining about the way Biblical words were

performed at St. Alban's. Modern distinctions between Evangelical denominations that define themselves as "Bible-based" and the more traditional practice of other groups may obscure the quantity of Biblical language embedded in the Anglican service that was being carried out by the ritualists. Before the Eucharist (with its "melodrama" style music) would have been a service of the Word, including a Psalm, readings from both Testaments, and a Gospel reading, and the Eucharistic service would have included Biblical passages such as the Sanctus, Benedictus, Kyrie and Gloria. Despite the suggestion that they ignored the Bible, often levelled at English-speaking churches with more Roman Catholic tendencies, the Holborn ritualists were carrying out a service crammed with Biblical material. Thus Shaftesbury's condemnations, though they sit within broader nineteenth-century controversies over theology, ecclesiastical authority and church history, are strongly concerned with the way Biblical material is being performed within the liturgy, though he might not have phrased it in that way. His criticism of "singing" and "screaming", can be placed alongside other suspicions of performances that obscure or distort the meaning of the text (and his reference to "clouds and clouds of incense" is also concerned with obscurity and camouflage, if more metaphorically).

Hughes' lack of patience for people who mispronounce the Bible when reading aloud finds a parallel, though with a distinctively different approach, in the writings of Irenaeus, the second-century Bishop of Lyons. In his attack on the Gnostic religious system in *Against Heresies*, Irenaeus becomes caught up in an argument over the phrase "the god of this world has blinded the minds of unbelievers", and whether it suggests that there is more than one divine being, as the Gnostics suggests. His solution is to argue that Paul's rhetorical style frequently involved transposing phrases within sentences, so that "the god of this world hath blinded the minds of unbelievers" should be better understood as "God hath blinded the minds of the unbelievers of this world". He suggests that his readers can come to appreciate this point by a practical demonstration involving reading aloud:

> For if anyone read the passage thus – according to Paul's custom, as I show elsewhere, and by many examples, that he uses transposition of words – "In whom God", then pointing it off, and making a slight interval, and at the same time read also the rest [of the sentence] in one [clause], "hath blinded

the minds of them of this world that believe not", he shall find out the true [sense]; that it is contained in the expression "God hath blinded the minds of the unbelievers of this world." And this is shown by means of the little interval [between the clause].

(183)

Irenaeus locates the true meaning of the Biblical passage in the way it sounds when it is read aloud with a certain pattern of pauses and articulation, and appeals to the hearers' own verbal recitation to back up his argument. In giving other examples of the way "the apostle frequently uses a transposed order in his sentences, due to the rapidity of his discourses, and the impetus of the Spirit which is in him", Irenaeus goes further in asserting the vital necessity of correct vocal performance (183). The doctrinal error that he attempts to correct in the "god of this world" passage is relatively subtle, so he produces a more obvious example, where ignoring the rhetorical style, and mangling it in performance, would result in a clear and drastic theological problem:

"And shall the wicked be revealed, whom the Lord Jesus Christ shall slay with the Spirit of His mouth, and shall destroy him with the presence of his coming; [even him] whose coming is after the working of Satan, with all power, and signs, and lying wonders." Now in these [sentences] the order of the words is thus: "And then shall be revealed that wicked, whose coming is after the working of Satan, with all power, and signs, and lying wonders, whom the Lord Jesus shall slay with the spirit of His mouth, and shall destroy with the presence of His coming." For he does not mean that the coming of the Lord is after the working of Satan; but the coming of the wicked one, who we also call Antichrist.

(184)

Satisfied that he has proved his point, Irenaeus relishes the clear demonstration that Paul uses this technique of verbal transposition, and the egregious error that would be caused by ignoring it:

If, then, one does attend to the [proper] reading [of the passage], and if he do not exhibit the intervals of breathing as they occur, there shall be not only incongruities, but also, when reading, he will utter blasphemy, as if the advent of the Lord could take place according to the working of Satan. So therefore, in such passages, the hyperbaton must be exhibited by the reading, and the apostle's meaning following on, preserved . . .

(184)

Irenaeus is as concerned as Kent Hughes that public reading should be effective, and carried out properly, but his approach is very different. Where Hughes noted problems in performance, and prescribed quiet personal study of the text on the page to solve them, Irenaeus notes a problem in the text, and prescribes vocal performance to solve it. Hughes assumes that meaning is located on the page, and understanding is a process that takes place between the solo reader and the text. This necessarily happens before a recitation, which is imagined as an act whereby meaning is reproduced seamlessly in public. Irenaeus seems to imagine performance as capable of producing meaning in itself, even correcting ambiguities and errors that might creep into a page-centred reading. For the Bishop of Lyons, meaning emerges in the breathing, the pauses and the emphases of the performer's voice. The Biblical text is less an entirely secure storehouse of meaning that a reader must select from and reproduce accurately, and more like the score of a piece of music, which needs to be transposed into a different medium via performance in order for its significance to unfold itself.

The rhetorical culture of the early centuries of Christianity could even produce a certain suspicion, or at least anxiety, around the act of personal reading. Augustine of Hippo's fourth century *Confessions* provide the first definite account of someone reading silently, in his description of his studies under Ambrose of Milan:

> But when he [Ambrose] was reading, his eyes scanned the page, and his heart explored the meaning, but his voice was silent and his tongue was still.

(114)

As Alberto Manguel points out, there are earlier possible indications of silent reading in sources by authors such as Plutarch and Euripides – and there is some controversy amidst scholars over just how rare the practice of silent reading might have been in the ancient world – but this habit of Ambrose's was sufficiently odd for Augustine to make a point of describing it. He not only mentions his master's habit of reading with "his voice . . . silent and his tongue . . . still", but goes on to justify the practice, speculating that "in the short time when he was free from the turmoil of other men's affairs and was able to refresh his own mind, he would not wish to be distracted" or that if he read aloud, he might be interrupted by students and slowed down:

> Perhaps he was afraid that, if he read aloud some obscure passage in the author he was reading might raise a question in the mind of an attentive listener, and he would then have to explain the meaning or even discuss some of the more difficult points.
>
> (114)

On a more practical level, Augustine wonders whether "Perhaps a more likely reason why he read to himself was that he needed to spare his voice, which quite easily became hoarse" (114). He ends the account with a curious remark: "But whatever his reason, we may be sure it was a good one" (114). Once again the assumptions behind the account are potentially more important than the statements it makes: Augustine assumes that some explanation will be necessary for Ambrose's behaviour. Reading silently is not just a little strange, but potentially unworthy of such a great person, and Augustine feels the need to assure his readers that whatever reason Ambrose had would have been worthy.

The context of the particular line about Ambrose's eyes gliding over the page appears to shed some light on Augustine's ambivalence. It comes in a sequence in which Augustine discusses gradually coming closer to Christian understanding, but notes how that process was frustrated at times by his inability to discuss faith directly and personally with Ambrose.

> I could not ask him the questions I wished to ask in the way that I wished to ask them, because so many people used to keep him busy with their problems that I was prevented from talking to him face to face. When he was not with them, which was never for very long at a time, he was reviving his body with the food that it needed, or refreshing his mind with reading.
>
> (113-4)

It is this situation that prompts his account of Ambrose's silent reading, which rather took some of his students aback:

All could approach him freely and it was not usual for visitors to be announced, so that often, when we came to see him, we found him reading like this, for he never read aloud. We would sit there quietly, for no-one had the heart to disturb him when he was so engrossed in study. After a time we went away again . . .

(114)

The explanation of the saint's quiet habits – and the assurance that his motivations must have been pure and serious – comes as justification for a practice that confused and even frustrated students, and Augustine "had no chance to probe the heart of this man, [God's] holy oracle . . . unless it was some matter that could be treated briefly" (114). He heard Ambrose on the Sabbath, "rightly expounding the Word of truth among the people", and believed that the saint demonstrated the possibility of resolving Augustine's doubts, but

As for his secret hopes, his struggles against the temptations which must come to one so highly placed, the consolations he found in adversity, and the joy he knew in the depths of his heart when he fed upon your Bread, these were quite beyond my surmise for they lay outside my experience. For his part he did not know how I was tormented or how deeply I was engulfed in danger.

(113)

The habit of sitting quietly and reading devotional works, which may look very familiar to modern Christians accustomed to Bible reading and daily "quiet time", comes close to a spiritual and pastoral failure in Augustine's anecdote. This is emphasised by the delicate echoes of the Pauline epistles in two of his lines. His description of hearing Ambrose "rightly expounding the Word of truth among the people" may contain a hint of the injunction in 2 Timothy 2:15 to study to appear before God as a worthy workman who handles and explains the Word of truth, whereas Augustine's frustration that he had no chance to ask the saint about his private faith and "the hope he bore within him" chimes with 1 Peter 3:15, with its instruction to "sanctify the Lord God in your hearts: and be ready always to give an answer to every man that asketh you a reason of the hope that is in you". Though one duty was clearly being carried out, there is a suggestion behind Augustine's praise (and defence) of the saint that Ambrose's behaviour made his student wonder whether the other injunction was being put into practice as successfully as could be wished.

Some explanation of Augustine's vague unease with the silent reading he found Ambrose engaged in can be found in the work of Walter J. Ong on the differences between "oral" and "literate" cultures. Ong's analysis of the ways language works in speech and writing, and the cultures who rely predominantly on each, reveals radical differences that went far beyond words being "contained" by the page or by speech out loud. The distinction shaped the entire way cultures conceived of knowledge, meaning and even whether "words" existed. For example, Ong notes that literature cultures tend to imagine words as existing visibly, as things which can be written down, left somewhere, and then picked back up again later. In oral cultures, words are more like activities, something that is being done, and which even whilst it is happening is slipping away. Words in such cultures are "a mode of action" rather than "the counter-sign of thought", and "it is not surprising that the Hebrew term *dabar* means 'word' and 'event'" (32). Another profound difference is revealed in the operations of the senses that we use to listen to spoken words and read written words: "Sight isolates, sound incorporates. Whereas sight situates the observer outside what he views, at a distance, sound pours into the hearer." (70) Readers sit next to each other, each in separate mental universes, but listeners become an audience, a whole group joined in attention, going through the same experience together, even sometimes (as happens at the theatre or cinema) breathing together. The written word encourages an analytic, dissecting mode of thought, in which knowledge is imagined as outside us, whereas spoken words encourage a unifying, harmonising mode that embodies meaning in experience.[1]

Ong's book mentions Augustine of Hippo in passing as a "savan[t] living in a culture that knew some literacy but still carried an overwhelmingly massive oral residue", and discusses the oral

---

1. Meaning can also be more personal when it is produced via speech. The *viva voce*, or oral examination, residually present in US and British higher education, is a remnant of the centuries when all examination was carried out via "disputation". Its use to examine the higher degrees (as well as sometimes to decide whether a candidate should be awarded a higher mark if they are on the borderline) displays a residual assumption that writing can be a way to detach meaning from a person, and to obscure their real knowledge, whereas in speech they can be truly searched and understood.

culture of Christianity at rather more length (36). He stresses the emphasis on speech and proclamation, mentioning that in Trinitarian theology God's Word is a living breathing presence rather than an inert thing, and that the "Spirit" which gives life to the dead "Letter" in 2 Corinthians is the same word as the breath of the mouth.

Ong's explanation of orality and literacy goes some way to unpacking the unease and even anxiety in Augustine's anecdote about his master. Though the Scriptures that Ambrose expounded were written texts, just like the devotional works his students found him writing, they still encoded a great deal of the oral culture in which they had emerged and which continued to surround their use. We can trace these in the image of God speaking the world into being (and only then "seeing" it afterwards), the stress in the prophetic writings on the "Word of the Lord" that arrives as speech and the emphasis in the New Testament on the Gospel as "kerygma" or "proclamation". Much early Christian practice was situated within this oral mode, to the extent that Ambrose's quiet devotional reading looked like a deliberate withdrawal from the community of his students, and an intentional closing them out from his consciousness as it focused on God. The distrust of outward performance and "theatre" that turns up in some modern Christian writing, as we saw earlier, is strikingly reversed here, in a suspicion of the inward spiritual landscape of silent reading.

Acting Out and Acting Up

In this chapter, I have deliberately chosen to present examples that will probably seem outlandish or even comic to many readers. I was certainly never told that Shakespeare should be kept away from actors at all costs, or that sitting quietly reading the Bible is a bit suspicious and not very Christian. Nonetheless, these were attitudes held by major figures within the history of Christianity and Shakespearean theatre. It is not really possible to dismiss Augustine of Hippo as a marginal crank who is irrelevant to the interpretation of the Bible, nor to suggest that Charles Lamb, William Hazlitt and Samuel Johnson just didn't "get" Shakespeare. Their attitudes can make us examine our own assumptions about the natural and right ways to read these books. They can also alert us to the traces that are left in our own cultural surroundings by the ideas and assumptions held by people in the past. We might not share Shaftesbury's visceral disgust at the chanting and bowing during a church service, but we are likely to have instinctive ideas about what constitutes a "proper" or "respectful" recitation of Bible verses at weddings or public memorial services (or whatever other texts we might prefer in those situations instead of the Bible). Performance continues to pose questions and problems to us in our interactions with these sacred texts. A description of Jesus' trial reads as a straightforward narrative when one person silently scans the page with their eye, but when it is performed during a service on Good Friday, with different readers taking the lines of the various characters, the congregation can experience it as a powerful moment of religious witnessing. Which of these is the "real" meaning? When two teenagers act out a scene from *A Midsummer Night's Dream*, and express their own emotional turmoil through the centuries-old lines, are they adding to the text or finding what was already there? These are not questions with easy answers, and they challenge our ideas about where meaning resides and how it is created.

5.

People of the Books

So far I have been exploring the textual history of Shakespeare and the Bible, their canonical shape and the modes via which they have been read and interpreted. In this chapter I shall examine some of the groups that lay claim to these books in the modern world. As has become clear in previous chapters, there is no obvious, natural or evident way to identify and fix the meanings within the Bible or the works of Shakespeare. A variety of groups and communities, from theatres to churches to universities, make claims about the correct way to read these books, and the authentic way to put their words into practice. In the following pages, I shall describe and analyse a few groups who present themselves as "people of the books", and consider how they use Shakespeare and the Bible to validate themselves and their own activities. This sometimes involves considerable controversy, and always involves a claim to wield the enormous authority that these texts possess in our culture.

Bible People and People's Bibles

The Biblical texts have been part of Christian communities' lives since the earliest days of the church, as we noticed in earlier chapters. From Jesus' reading of the prophecies of Isaiah recorded in the Gospels, through the meetings Justin Martyr describes as listening to "the memoirs of the apostles", to medieval monks chanting the Psalms, the texts that make up the Bible have been a major focus for Christians' self-understanding and identity as a group. The debates over the correct way to interpret it, and which communities or institutions have the right to rule authoritatively on its use and meaning, have been equally significant in Christian history. There is a dialogue between Christian groups and the Bible, in which the identities of both are partly defined by the other. As the chapter on canonicity explored, the Bible as we have it today (in the various modern forms) arose from the life and controversies of the churches. In turn, reading and preaching the Bible shapes the identity of the churches. Christian groups in modern society validate and justify themselves on the grounds of their connection with the Bible. Particularly in the Evangelical tradition, Christian writing is full of casual references to the Bible, a rhetorical gesture that validates the speaker and their activities by aligning them with Scripture. For example, the website of the Evangelical Alliance, an organisation that campaigns on behalf of British evangelicals, carries an "About Us" section which mentions that:

> Unity is what drives us – but not just for unity's sake. By bringing people together, we are following the John 17 mandate to show the immense love of God, who sent his Son for us.

This is not part of a resource pack or an article on the theological justification for political activity on behalf of the Christian communities in Britain (both of which the Evangelical Alliance could supply). It appears in the group's explanation of itself, tying their activities as an organisation not only to a Christian account of the world but to a specific Bible verse. It is also significant that the Bible verse is not quoted verbatim, but referred to by a reference. The seventeenth chapter of John's Gospel is Jesus' prayer identifying his followers and asking for protection and sanctification for them, but the website mentions the passage in shorthand as if every reader will know its basic outline. In doing so, the Evangelical Alliance identify themselves in another way with reference to the Bible: they are not only the sorts of followers for whom Jesus prayed in this passage, but they are the sort of Christians who quote the Bible easily and confidently, and expect others to be able to do the same. The very off-hand nature of the reference acts as a gentle shibboleth, signalling to both those who can mentally look the passage up and those who can't that this website is for and about Bible-literate people.

In a similar vein, a local church might state on its website that it offers "clear Bible teaching", a student group might be advised to seek out "a Bible-believing church" whilst at university, or a pastor might recommend a book to his congregation as "strong Bible Christianity". All of these relate to the connection between the Biblical texts and Christianity, but "Bible" is functioning here as much as a marker of identity as a literal description. After all, an

Anglo-Catholic service such as the one described with horror by Lord Shaftesbury in a previous chapter, replete with chanting, incense, bowing and Latin, would contain a large number of Biblical words. "Bible", when used in "Bible teaching" or "Bible believing", is a term groups use to define themselves within the spectrum of modern Christianity. When the pastor and teacher John Stott declared that Evangelicals were "Bible people", he did not mean to distinguish them from those who looked to the Qur'ān or the Guru Granth Sahib for their religious guidance. His statement was intended – and understood – to mark out Evangelicals from the Catholic and Liberal traditions within English-speaking Christianity.

Similarly the use of "Bible" in the title of "Bible Colleges" such as Moody Bible Institute and Biola University (whose name was previously an acronym for the Bible Institute of Los Angeles) signals both more and less than the subject matter of their courses. Students taking degrees at these institutions may study a range of subjects, including theology, mission, sociology, music, sport and education, and will not simply be instructed in Biblical Studies. "Bible" here does not designate the material that will be covered or the knowledge that the students will possess when they graduate. It is more likely to imply a general ethos and attitude to the purposes of education itself, signalling a view of the world that sees Biblical authority as paramount. A Bible College is less likely to be an institution that only offers teaching on the contents of the Biblical texts, than it is to be a college that has rhetorically placed itself under the sovereignty of the Bible. The book's name acts as an equivalent of the "National", "Royal", or "Free" in the title of other schools and colleges, and in fact implies a much stronger link between the origins and the purposes of the institution. Attending or teaching at a Bible College involves (at least nominally) joining an organisation that has designated the Bible as its governing authority, however much such colleges might diverge from each other in practice. This can be highlighted by the comparison with an Agricultural College or Music College, or a College of Liberal Arts: all of these are likely to have some institutional ethos, but their names do not present a specific ideological allegiance. Thus the use of "Bible" as an adjective or an affiliation is often a validation of a particular ideology or institution, rather than being intended as a neutral description. Declaring allegiance can often be a way of claiming legitimacy within a particular tradition, and putting oneself (or one's institution) under the authority of the Bible can

act as a claim that others are misusing or misinterpreting it. This
is particularly the case for many Bible colleges, since a number of
them were founded in the early twentieth century as a reaction
to the perceived liberalism of the mainstream denominations and
their training institutions. At least during their founding, the
claim that they were Bible colleges involved implying that other
colleges did not recognise the Bible's authority, or implement its
vision of the world.

The late twentieth century saw a disagreement over the question
posed in the title of Philip Davies' book, *Whose Bible Is It Anyway?*,
which pointed up the way in which institutional claims about
faithfulness to the Bible can also operate as claims of validation for
the institution and its particular reading of the texts. The increasing
movement of US and British public culture towards secularism,
coupled with the rapid development of academic theories of
interpretation that had no explicitly religious basis, led many to feel
that the Bible no longer "belonged" to the Christian churches. The
debate coalesced around two possible groups who now "owned"
the Bible: the religious communities and the secular universities. In
practice, of course, this is a drastic simplification. Many churches
contain acute Biblical critics whose sceptical and careful practice
in dealing with the texts does not prevent them from engaging
wholeheartedly in religious worship, and the academic study of
the Bible in universities is often carried out by people with deep
spiritual convictions about the ultimate significance of these texts.
However, the debate tended to be framed in terms of whether the
Bible properly belonged on the lectern of a church or the desk of
a university. The vigour of this disagreement highlights one of the
central themes of this book: that the meaning which emerges from
texts is hugely influenced by how they are read, in all senses of that
word. The question of who owns the Bible is the question of how
it should be read.

One side of the debate is represented by a collection of essays
entitled *Reclaiming the Bible for the Church* and the introductory
chapter contributed by the editors, Carl E. Braaten and Robert W.
Jenson. They state that "what needs to be reclaimed for the church
is the Bible as authoritative Scripture", an idea which for them had
been eroded by the dominance of historical-critical scholarship (x).
The close historical study of the Biblical texts has, in their view,
"tended to take over the entire operation of biblical interpretation",
with the result that religious faith has been "marginalized" and the

"unity of the Bible" when viewed from a Christian perspective has been unpicked into "a multiplicity of unrelated fragments" (x). Braaten and Jenson are particularly critical of the claims of academic critics to values of objectivity and neutrality. Whilst historical-critical interpreters claim to be simply reading what is there in the text, unhindered by prior assumptions or dogma about the religious meaning of the text, so that their work achieves "the status of objective historical science", nonetheless "it is possible to show that historical critics approach the text with their own set of prior commitments", which can be "linked to ideologies alien or hostile to the faith of the Christian church" (xi). Countering the suggestion that religious readers of the Bible had their vision distorted by their prior beliefs in its significance, they argued that supposedly "objective" critics also brought their own presuppositions to the text. Jenson and Braaten were probably thinking of the influence of Marxism, feminism and other strands of critical theory that had such an effect on English-speaking universities during the 1970s and 1980s. They sum up their position thus:

> Which hermeneutic, then, is best qualified to understand the Scriptures? That of the autonomous scholar whose private ideological commitment is disguised as objective scientific research, or that of a community of faithful memory that forthrightly acknowledges the Scriptures as divinely inspired authority?
>
> (xi)

The opposite position is represented by Philip Davies, who draws an equally rigid boundary between the spheres of academic and religious interpretation, whilst remaining on the other side. To him, "confessional" or believing interpretation of the Biblical texts and academic study of them are "fundamentally quite different types of behaviour" and even entirely different disciplines. He allows a thoroughgoing "right" of theological interpretation to the Christian churches, but as a way of limiting that kind of interpretation only to believing communities. Davies accepts that "the religious institutions and communities of Judaism and Christianity have a claim on their bibles and declares that the "claim is valid within those communities" but denies their right "to try and universalize it" to control the interests of those who study Biblical texts for artistic, cultural or historical reasons" (13). Whilst:

there is a need to articulate the role and meaning of the scriptures in the context of Judaism and Christianity, so there is no realistic hope of imposing an ecclesial interpretation outside the ecclesial domain.

(14)

Davies is concerned about saving the potential meanings that these texts may have contained for the writer, or may produce for the reader, from the meddling of the centuries in the middle:

Whatever communication may be possible between writer and reader via private reading of the text cannot be censored or controlled by an intervening history of ecclesiastical reading . . . no ancient writer should have his or her text accorded a retrospective meaning dictated by the dogmatic requirements of an institution which chose to "canonize" it.

(14)

He is happy to cede the right of the church to carry on its own "discourse . . . about its scriptures" but only because that discourse should be limited to "the church domain" (14).

Though I have presented them as opposing sides of the debate, these critics draw somewhat similar lines in their attempt to distinguish the correct sites in which to understand the Biblical texts. Davies may be an atheist wishing to "save" the Christian Bible from the tyranny and censorship of the churches, and Jenson and Braaten may be devout believers concerned with keeping the "hostile" and "alien" theories of historical-critical interpretation from distorting the correct interpretation of the Scriptures. Nonetheless, they all depict a situation in which there are two clearly defined spheres of interpretation, in which thoroughly distinct methods of reading are carried out for drastically different ends.

Perhaps they have more in common than first appears, and the real opposition to these attitudes is provided by Francis Watson in his book *Text, Church and World*. Watson argues for a theologically-informed Biblical criticism, and a critically-informed church discourse, suggesting that though there has been "a recent vogue for interdisciplinary work of various kinds", he is unusual in "advocat[ing] a renewed dialogue with systematic theology" as a route towards new insights for Biblical scholars (vii). He counters the rigid separation between church and academy that appears in Davies, Braaten and Jenson with two major points.

Firstly, he denies the simple and controlling quality of theological discourse that they seem to assume. He shows, via discussion of "law" and "gospel" in the thought of Luther, and the representation of women in the Bible, that a theological discussion of the Biblical texts which takes place within Christian orthodoxy has resources with which to criticise and evaluate those texts themselves. For Watson, interpreting the Bible "within the church", reading it in a distinctively Christian sense, does not and cannot mean simply repeating the words of the text and "believing" them in a straightforward sense. Those words are troubling, complex and multivalent, and a Christian reading will be alert to the moments when they counter or critique the apparent meaning of other parts of the Bible.

Text, Church and World also rejects the rigid lines drawn between Christian and "secular" ways of interpreting the Bible, which the critics above are keen on. It is part of Watson's model of interpretation that "insights originating in the secular world outside the Christian community" are valuable and even essential. It is a mistake, in his reading, to "regard the church as a self-sufficient sphere closed off from the world", and Watson suggests that the Holy Spirit "blows where it will" when it comes to inspiring and enabling the true understanding of the Bible. This account of how theological and academic approaches to the Bible relate to each other does not seek a moderate line between two extremes, but questions the assumptions made by those who argue for the demarcation of appropriately Christian and appropriately secular spheres of reading. In doing so, Watson rejects precisely the elements that scholars from both sides of the debate have in common.

Thus the discussion over the "ownership" of the texts, as expressed in the method of reading them, does not simply break down into two sides, with a group of pastors and believers on one side, and a group of scholars and lecturers on the other, both insisting that theirs is the only meaning to be taken from the text. It is often a question of how a text has been handled, and whose principles it has been read upon, which causes controversy. These questions, which might seem rather abstruse when discussed in the academic tone of the scholars I have just cited, sometimes come into sharp focus in public controversy. A recent example is provided by a letter published in the student newspaper *The Sewanee Purple*, written by a Professor Paul Holloway of that university, after an honorary doctorate was awarded to N. T. Wright. Holloway's criticism of Sewanee's decision to bestow this award focused on the idea that Wright was not a scholar, and so should not be recognised by a degree that attributed academic authority to the recipient. In Holloway's provocative terms:

> My complaint is that Sewanee has recognized Wright as a scholar in my discipline, when in fact he is little more than a book-a-year apologist. Wright comes to the evidence not with honest questions but with ideologically generated answers that he seeks to defend. I know of no critical scholar in the field who trusts his work. He contradicts what I stand for professionally as well as the kind of hard-won intellectual integrity I hope to instill in my students. I feel like the professor of biology who has had to sit by and watch a Biblical creationist receive an honorary degree in science.

Earlier in the letter Holloway criticised Wright's writings on the subject of sexuality, calling them "offensive and harmful", but his major objection was not based on any repudiation of Wright's theological or political views. It was based instead on his charge that those views – a particular form of Evangelical Protestantism – determined the processes and outcomes of his work on the Bible. Holloway does not only suggest that Wright's conclusions are wrong, but that those conclusions are the starting-point of his discussion of the Bible, rather than the outcome of an open and unbiased investigation of the evidence and previous scholarship.

This letter was itself the subject of vigorous criticism, both from within the Sewanee student and alumni body and from the wider world of Christian scholarship and church life. During the controversy that followed, various proofs were advanced for Wright's suitability (or otherwise) as a scholar, including his publication record, the profundity of his insights, and his current academic position as Professor of New Testament and Early Christianity at the University of St. Andrews. Holloway's ensuing defence of his letter claimed that Wright had ruled himself out of the role of scholar during an interview he gave to *The Gospel Coalition*. Wright's reply to a question on Scriptural authority included the following passage:

> Well, in terms of method, sola Scriptura is what I've always tried to do, basically. You could put it negatively . . . If you find yourself thinking down a track where you think, Oh, well, if I

go there, that'll mean ditching this bit of the Bible or that bit, then all sorts of warning lights flash and say, "You probably shouldn't be going there!"

(in Wax)

Having cited these words, Holloway evidently considered his strictures to have been proved, declaring that this admission invalidated Wright's supporters' claims for his scholarship, since they represented a specific way in which he limited his own critical work on theological grounds.

> How often do these warning lights flash in Wright's head? How often do his academic sensibilities yield to his Biblicism? There is no way to know, since there are no footnotes saying, "My warning lights just went off again."

The objections Holloway posed to Wright's official recognition as a New Testament scholar, and his reply to the arguments which Wright's supporters had marshalled in defence of his degree, echoed the account James Barr gave in the late 1970s of the way fundamentalist Christians misread the work of conservative scholars (who were themselves erudite and painstaking professionals). For one of these readers:

> [t]he function of conservative scholarship is to give him comfort and security, assuring him that the certainties of his religion will not be put in question. He has this comfort and security, however, because he does not really understand how the conservative scholar really works.

(123)

The average fundamentalist, according to Barr, reads conservative scholarly books because they tend to survey the range of critical opinions available and then endorse an opinion that accords with the religious beliefs of the reader. For example, a particular work may give the opinion that the Gospels date from earlier in the years after Jesus' death than other scholars would believe, and that they contain more reliable evidence for the life and sayings of Jesus than most professors might think. This might be taken by the reader as an endorsement of their theological system and their own religious practices. However, as Barr points out, a scholarly method admits of the possibility of error, and bases its judgement upon the balance of evidence and the best available interpretations. In surveying the current scholarly positions, such a work commits itself to operating on the same basic principles that produced those positions. It would, for Barr, be operating in intellectual bad faith to use the evidence of Biblical critics to bolster or prove a particular religious position, when that position would not be altered if the evidence available changed, or was persuasively shown to indicate a different conclusion. In engaging with critical scholarship, and endorsing certain critical conclusions, Barr considers such authors to have implicitly accepted the common basis of scholarly investigation, tacitly agreeing that not only the results of that investigation are correct, but that they are correct because of the processes that led to them. For a preacher or a believer, the Virgin birth, the resurrection or the death of John the Baptist may be true as part of a religious system, but for a historical scholar they are valid conclusions insofar as they are arrived at by commonly agreed historiographical methods. Holloway's charge against Wright is that he operates in a methodological grey area, apparently framing his questions, and carrying out the subsequent analysis, according to the imperatives of contemporary New Testament studies, but in fact beginning "with ideologically generated answers that he then seeks to defend". To state the obvious, it is not reading the Bible theologically (or in one particular religious tradition) that Holloway objects to, but to doing so whilst (according to him) claiming to be engaged in dispassionate and neutral historical enquiry that just happens to produce exactly the results needed to defend existing dogma.[1]

---

1. It is for this reason that comments on Holloway's second piece, which sought to defend Wright's reputation by arguing that he is less of an inerrantist than this interview made him sound, might be regarded as missing the point. The inerrancy of Scripture, when phrased in that way, is a question of doctrine, not of historical investigation. It refers to a certain theological principle, not to an empirical hypothesis that has been posited about the Bible's references to certain matters in the outside world. "Inerrancy" is a theological question, not one that the sort of New Testament scholarship Holloway engages in can address. It may be that historical, archaeological and sociological evidence has caused many Christians to modify their doctrine of the infallibility of Scripture, in the face of changing attitudes about the relationship between the Bible and the world. But doing so was a theological adjustment, and Holloway would no doubt argue that saying Wright is less of an inerrantist than this "warning lights" passage makes him sound is to propose something about Wright's theological positions, not his scholarly practice.

Shakespeare and His Disputed Inheritance

A great number of institutions carry out their business "in the name of Shakespeare", to borrow Gary Taylor's phrase, and I would like to focus on two in particular here (6). Both bear the name of Shakespeare, and use it in a variety of ways. The Shakespeare Birthplace Trust in Stratford-upon-Avon and Shakespeare's Globe in London are both major tourist destinations, both involved in educating people about Shakespeare's life and historical context, and both part of the wider "Shakespeare industry".

The Shakespeare Birthplace Trust is, as the name suggests, an organisation centred on the house where the playwright was born, which was purchased for this purpose in the 1840s. Today the Trust involves educational activities, a significant research library that holds the archives of the Royal Shakespeare Company, and other heritage elements including other buildings in Stratford and a farm. It nonetheless retains its name, and the association with the house. The meaning ascribed to that house is not exactly clear; its importance seems to have been originally part of the particular nineteenth-century veneration of "great men", and almost certainly owed something to the Victorian interest in origins. Robin Gilmour has suggested that the public culture of this era was painfully aware of its own modernity, feeling itself to be a "parvenu civilization", and thus was attracted to heraldry, origin myths, heritage and other markers of belonging that could tie them to the past (1). Visiting the historical site where Shakespeare himself had his origin sits comfortably within this approach to the past, though from a modern point of view, Stratford does not really represent the most interesting part of Shakespeare's life. It was not the site of his theatrical involvement or his literary output, and though it was no doubt formative for his later life there is very little that actually happened to Shakespeare in Stratford that connects to his fame. To put it rather bluntly, Shakespeare grew up in a small town and left it when he was a young man in search of the opportunities offered by London. When he had made his money as a playwright, he returned to the small town, bought one of the biggest houses and settled down to a retirement which involved (amongst other things) taking his neighbours to court and buying up grain in order to make a profit when the harvest was bad. The elements of Shakespeare's life that actually took place in Stratford-upon-Avon are not those from which to construct a heroic historical icon, nor a cultural behemoth. This is not to suggest that there is no value in visiting Stratford-upon-Avon, nor that the Birthplace Trust does not do immensely valuable work in preserving historical buildings and making them available to the public, not to mention their provision of archives to scholars and educational days for school students. It is worth noticing, though, that the apparently natural activity of setting up an institution that preserves the house where Shakespeare was born has no necessary connection with the reasons he is famous. The Birthplace Trust might be thought of as a focal point where the international cultural prestige of Shakespeare becomes attached to a historical site. The desire to understand Shakespeare's words, and to get closer to his mind, fastens on the places and relics he left behind. The Birthplace Trust's slogan "Shakespeare Lives Here" puns on the association between the domestic buildings and the variety of activities – from displays of falconry, to the publication of a Tudor Cookbook, to an online education course – through which Shakespeare's works and world are "brought alive". It demonstrates the blurring seen elsewhere in this book between a person, a collection of books, an artistic activity, a historical period and a quality of culture, all gathered under one word: "Shakespeare".

Shakespeare's Globe is the end result of a project begun by the American actor and director Sam Wanamaker to reconstruct the sort of theatre Shakespeare wrote for in roughly the same location. In the longer term, it was the result of the sort of stage-centred criticism of Shakespeare that was discussed in a previous chapter, an approach to the plays that stresses the importance of performance in truly understanding them. This was a process begun by insights of William Poel and the Elizabethan Stage Society, who insisted on restoring the scripts from their rearranged Victorian versions, and performing them without the cumbersome stage machinery and bombastic set pieces that had wrenched them out of shape. The idea that the right way to appreciate a Shakespeare play was to get inside it, to produce it as closely to the conditions under which Shakespeare wrote as possible, took a hundred years to come to full fruition. The theatre, which opened in the 1990s, was variously greeted as a theatrical laboratory, a truly authentic site for Shakespearean performance, a continuation of the Poel tradition, and a Disneyfied tourist trap. One scholarly description of the project suggested that it could reconnect audiences with the past via theatrical tradition, using the plays in their authentic settings to revitalise the traces of past experience in the scripts:

> To play *King Lear* in a rebuilt Globe is to call on an audience's mind, by spatial and visual means as well as verbal, a world now gone but nevertheless, even if changed, also accessible through the scripts of its plays.
>
> (in Mulryne and Shewring, 24)

Of course, this theatrical experience is very different from the theatrical experiences undergone by people at the turn of the seventeenth century. There are physical differences: the site is clean, well-maintained and safe, unlike the crowded and relatively dirty conditions of the early modern public playhouses. Perhaps even more significant in terms of the artistic experience is the radical difference in what theatre means within modern culture. For Shakespeare's audience it was a disreputable and barely legal form of entertainment, denounced by the Church, under threat from city business interests, and subject to sneers from literary figures like Sir Philip Sidney, who called the theatre of his age "neither of honest civility, nor skilful poetry" (243). Attending the theatre today – especially to see a Shakespeare play – is a conscious act of engagement with centuries of culture, which signals a certain level of education and appreciation of high arts. But a less noticeable difference, if perhaps equally significant, is the name of the theatre itself. No-one in late sixteenth-century London attended a theatre called Shakespeare's Globe, and a large proportion of the audience probably did not know on any given afternoon who had written the play they were watching.

The use of the playwright's name in the theatre's title reveals that the new performance space is not purely an institution setting out to explore theatrical history, but part of the modern Shakespeare industry. It both signals to potential audience members the kind of plays they can expect to see, and identifies itself with the cultural icon who epitomises artistic seriousness. It surely also indicates to the vast numbers of tourists who visit London that this theatre will provide an authentically "British" experience, equivalent to visiting the Tower of London or the Houses of Parliament in its summing up of the nation's heritage. The name designates the business brand of the theatre, as well as the major part of its repertory. It also acts as a focus around which Shakespeare's Globe organises its artistic exploration of the past. The "world now gone", which can be accessed via performances of King Lear according to the quotation above, is filtered and refracted through the work of one particular playwright, and the subsequent history of performance and interpretation which has gathered around his name. To the casual theatregoer or tourist passing Shakespeare's Globe on the south bank, the name both offers the richness of the past that can be experienced through the theatre and guarantees the authenticity of it. The past as filtered through Shakespeare is reliable and meaningful in a way that Noel Coward or Hans Christian Andersen could not guarantee.

The theatre's website describes the institution and its project thus:

> Shakespeare's Globe is a unique international resource dedicated to the exploration of Shakespeare's work and the playhouse for which he wrote, through the connected means of performance and education.
>
> ("About Us")

Alongside the theatre productions, there is the "Globe Exhibition and Tour" and a "Globe Education" section, all of which "seek to further the experience and international understanding of Shakespeare in performance". Globe Education is involved in academic research at the highest level, hosting research fellows and engaging with international scholars; another aspect of the theatre that sets it apart from most entertainment venues in Britain. Shakespeare's Globe is part of the complex system in which Shakespeare's name and works produce cultural authority. The theatre – like the Birthplace Trust – has a certain mystique because of its historical location, rather like a pilgrimage site. Performing Shakespeare is a mark of legitimacy for any theatre, a sign that they are capable of reproducing the most famous part of the English-language theatrical tradition. Doing so in a theatre that explicitly sets out to perform the plays in a building that approximates the one in which they first appeared works as an even stronger claim to authenticity. However the actors and scholars of Shakespeare's Globe might individually understand their artistic projects, there is no doubt that the Globe's shows are interpreted by many people as "proper" Shakespeare. This is validated by the box office figures, the media attention and the academic papers written about their work. In turn, the theatre's success as an artistic endeavour, a tourist attraction and an academic institution (none of which are mutually exclusive) continues to bolster the public image of Shakespeare as a cultural icon.

There has not been such a dramatic and explicit disagreement over who "owns" Shakespeare as there has been over the Bible in recent decades. There certainly are two sets of institutions that interpret Shakespeare's works in different modes – the theatre and the university – but as we have seen, the trend of the twentieth century was towards convergence between the two. Stage-centred criticism, in its various forms, was close to being the critical orthodoxy in university departments by the end of the century, and many theatre directors drew freely on insights developed in university study for their work. The comparatively abstruse approaches adopted by critical theorists in areas like deconstruction may not have had much of an impact on theatre practice, but there were few official splits between the theatres and the universities which resulted in manifestos or conferences. It is certainly fair to say, from anecdotal evidence, that theatre work and theatre reviewing has sometimes included a certain dismissive attitude to "ivory towers" and the "impractical ideas" that issue from departments of literary studies, as contrasted with the practical truths that become evident whilst actually staging the plays and asking people to pay money to watch. But this has not been generally codified into a recognised crisis within the field, or led to widespread denunciations of the "other camp".

One striking and controversial exception centres on techniques of "First Folio acting" developed by the actor, director and writer Patrick Tucker, who became famous for his Shakespeare productions employing the First Folio texts. Tucker's extensive work on the Folio, and the successful productions that resulted, has led him to advocate for it as the most "authentic" and most "theatrical" text available. His approach to performance arose from his experiences of productions that experimented with rehearsal and performance techniques which approximated as closely as possible to those used by Shakespeare's company. In his *Secrets of Acting Shakespeare*, Tucker recounts being at a meeting of the committee created to design and build Shakespeare's Globe in London, and finding that the famous "professors" present were stumped when asked a basic question about Elizabethan rehearsal times. Throughout the book he pours scorn on textual scholars and academics, who, he suggests, think they know better than Shakespeare, and advises actors to submit to the authority of Shakespeare himself as transmitted through the First Folio. The academics, a "high priesthood of scholars" who have "claimed guardianship of the plays", are depicted as scared by the clarity and common sense of simply reading what Shakespeare wrote, as it would threaten the smokescreen of complexity and nuance with which they persuade the public that they need professional scholars to interpret the text for them (84). As will be obvious from that brief quotation, Tucker's tone can often draw on the sort of polemical imagery more often associated with religious reform, and his account of high priests forcing mumbo-jumbo on the people for their own benefit taps into long strains of anticlericalism that sit near the surface of an Anglo-American culture which was shaped so strongly by nineteenth-century Protestantism. He has described the way his work "seems to make some people very angry", and that revealing the "secrets" to which his title refers has resulted in academics "shouting . . . that I am completely wrong and that the Folio is riddled with errors and not an authentic text to work from" (229).

Tucker's deliberately provocative approach to Shakespeare's texts has certainly produced a violent reaction in some established scholars. In his own sympathetic book on the First Folio movement, Don Weingust recounts that "At least one of the proponents of these First Folio techniques has been branded as 'the devil' by at least one important textual scholar", and that when it became known that he was researching the topic, "one well-known scholar emphatically urged me to 'blow them up'" (ix). A more critical account of Tucker's ideas, given by Anthony Dawson, suggests that the practitioners who follow First Folio acting are after "a sense of being in direct communication with some quasi-mystical and deeply authoritative voice from the past, indeed with Shakespeare himself" (149). This points towards the reason why so many scholars may be so hostile to the movement (aside from the aspersions that Tucker has cast on their learning and even the moral integrity of their profession): it draws on academic research for ends that have little to do with the principles of that research. Tucker's rationale for following all the punctuation, spellings and lineation of the First Folio authenticates itself by reference to historical investigation of the conditions under which Shakespeare's theatre company rehearsed and performed. In a theatre where actors only had a copy of their own part (rather than the whole play) and did not have the long, discussion-based rehearsals available to modern performers, the construction of the play itself guided the resulting performance to a greater extent. Tucker uses this to argue that the scripts contain Shakespeare's own stage directions and intentions for how the plays should be performed, "encoded" into the textual details of the First Folio. Where textual scholars see a web of historical circumstances in which Shakespeare's plays were shaped by the surrounding institutions and working conditions, Tucker detects the personal authority and mandate of the single genius.

Neither modern literary criticism nor performance scholarship are usually concerned with instructing people to "do what you are told by the author", but this is one of the central secrets encapsulated in *The Secrets of Acting Shakespeare* (218).

A parallel can be drawn between this controversy and Paul Holloway's criticism of N. T. Wright: some critics appear to feel that Tucker is using apparently academic methods in order to come to conclusions that put him beyond the scope of those methods. It is not that he comes to conclusions with which they disagree (that the First Folio, on balance, provides the most reliable or most theatrically viable text of most plays in the canon), but that his conclusions are not susceptible to academic discussion (that the First Folio transmits Shakespeare's personal intentions, which readers should obey).

People of the Books

This chapter has only been able to survey a few institutions and a couple of controversies, but they illustrate a larger situation in which both Shakespeare and the Bible are claimed by institutions in the contemporary world. In the process of using these books – teaching, performing and putting them into practice – groups such as churches, colleges and theatres identify themselves as the authoritative interpreters of the books' meanings. A college that adopts the Bible into its name not only implies something about the principles that will inform the education available there, but also uses the Bible to validate its own ethos and attitudes. When someone claims to be a "Biblical" preacher or a "Shakespearean" actor, they make a claim to legitimacy, declaring that their way of embodying these texts is authentic and in keeping with their true meaning. It also implies that other people's embodiment or enactment of the texts is less authentic. There is a complex interplay between the ways Shakespeare and the Bible inform and guide the groups which seek to put them into practice, and the ways those groups use the texts to invest themselves with the marks of authority. Despite that complexity, the process and its effects can be seen all over English-speaking cultures.

6.
Calling on Their Name:
Quotation and Appropriation

In English-speaking cultures that are increasingly diverse religiously and less defined by a single literary canon, Shakespeare and the Bible maintain a powerful presence in the language and symbols used for a variety of purposes. The institution of the British and American heads of state both continue to involve the presence of Biblical words, though in strikingly different ways: the material artefact sworn upon during the presidential inauguration; and the singing of the coronation anthem *Zadok the Priest*, which relates the anointing of King David. Shakespeare is used in political speeches, business training courses, and adverts for almost everything from fishing tackle to real estate to tractors. Though there are frequent complaints from traditionalists that people – particularly students – don't know their Bible or their Shakespeare these days, their continuing appearance in these spheres demonstrates that they carry some kind of commercial or political value. This chapter will explore quotations, echoes or references to the texts in contexts beyond religion or literature. As with the previous chapter, I won't be providing a history of these, or a survey of the fields where they are used in the present, but picking out a handful of examples. I will analyse these to see how they work and what effect they produce, paying attention to the purposes for which the allusions are being used. This should help readers in beginning to take apart the Biblical and Shakespearean echoes that surround them in modern culture, subjecting them to the same sort of sceptical attention.

The Powers That Be

The Bible has a prominent place in the state ceremonies of both Britain and the United States of America, though in rather different ways. The inauguration of a US President famously involves the swearing of an oath of office with one hand on the Bible. Though this does not involve reading any words from the volume, or mentioning any of the contents, it still carries implications about their meaning and significance. To swear on a Bible involves a tacit assumption about its value and weight, implying that it would be a more serious matter to break this oath than another, since it has somehow acquired solemnity by the presence of the book. It uses the volume more as a talisman than collection of writings, a physical symbol that stands for the faith and seriousness of the act. It would make no difference to the effectiveness of the oath what translation of the Bible it happened to be, nor if the Apocrypha were included. Not every president has used a Bible: John Quincy Adams used a law book and Lyndon Johnson swore on a Roman Catholic mass book, and neither were considered invalid presidents. Indeed, the tenuous connection between the swearing of the oath of office and the actual words of the Bible might be demonstrated by citing a passage from one of the most famous pieces of religious teaching it contains, the Sermon on the Mount in the Gospel of Matthew:

> Again, you have heard that it was said to those of ancient times, "You shall not swear falsely, but carry out the vows you have made to the Lord". But I say to say, Do not swear at all, either by heaven, for it is the throne of God, or by the earth, for it is his footstool, or by Jerusalem, for it is the city of the great King. And do not swear by your head, for you cannot make one hair white or black. Let your word be "Yes, Yes" or "No, No": anything more than this comes from the evil one.
>
> (5:33-7)

Many Christians do swear political and judicial oaths, and a great deal of thought has been expended on how this can be reconciled with the Sermon on the Mount, but there is an irony in using a book that contains Matthew's Gospel to swear an oath which highlights the gap between the verbal details of the text and the purpose to which it is being put. It isn't entirely disconnected from the meaning of the book as a whole, though. In this context, the Bible is being associated with the authority and legitimacy of the state by its involvement in the inauguration ceremony. It is both lending an air of continuity by its presence as an ancient text, and bestowing an air of the transcendent on the moment. For many citizens of the United States who are Christian believers, it also acts to focus the nation's mission and destiny. Despite the many controversies over America's status as a "Christian nation", and the details of history, the presence of the Bible in this ceremony acts as a visual symbol of the connection between Christianity and the state. However, it is remarkably unclear precisely what that connection might be, or which of the multiple possible connections is being affirmed. Does the Bible signify the centrality of Christian culture to the continuing health and prosperity of the American state? Or the historical religious traditions from which US democracy emerged, and which it acknowledges as its prehistory, just as the ceremony asserts the greater importance of popular legitimacy and secular pluralism? Might it even be read as a reminder of the fervour and strife of sixteenth-century religious politics, which in US popular political narrative led the Pilgrims and Founding Fathers to seek freedom across the seas, and which functions as a dialectical symbol of everyone's right to believe whatever they like in America, however outdated or apparently irrational? Possibly to some it represents nothing more (or nothing less) than the personal religious convictions of the President who is sworn in on this book, showing that to them this was a convenient and powerful way to bind their conscience to the duties of their office. Perhaps a significant part of the Bible's function in this ceremony is its ambiguity, and the way it allows people with widely differing political and religious convictions to use the inauguration ceremony as a focus of their civic devotion. Not unlike the American Constitution, the Bible in the inauguration may draw some of its value from the potential for people who totally disagree to think it affirms what they see as truly American values.

There is an equivalent use of the Bible in the state ceremonies of the United Kingdom, in the choral anthems by Handel that have been sung at the coronations of every monarch since George II's ascension to the throne in 1727. They are musical settings of particular passages of the Bible which had been used in previous coronation ceremonies, and the most famous is entitled *Zadok the Priest*, which runs thus:

Zadok the priest
And Nathan the prophet
Anointed Solomon king
And all the people
Rejoiced, rejoiced, rejoiced
And all the people
Rejoiced, rejoiced, rejoiced

Rejoiced, rejoiced, rejoiced
And all the people
Rejoiced, rejoiced, rejoiced and said:

God save the king
Long live the king
God save the king
May the king live forever
Amen, amen, alleluia, alleluia, amen, amen
Amen, amen, alleluia, amen.

When stripped of Handel's majestic musical setting, and the fervor of massed choirs on a historic occasion, this anthem may seem to be spreading a rather small passage of the Bible over a rather large area. Certainly to a skeptical (or republican) mind, these two verses show an almost neurotic emphasis on the delight of the people in welcoming their sovereign, and the secure consensus that had been established around how much everyone is looking forward to being thoroughly ruled for as long as possible. Not to mention that anyone with a working knowledge of the narratives the Old Testament contains about kings and their relationship with God and their people might wonder how appropriate it is to borrow a passage from them to celebrate the legitimacy of a British monarch.

Thus if this is approached as a Bible reading, it might appear both rather light on content, and a little unconvincing in its certainty about the divine approval of kings and their doings it presents. However, approached as a creative appropriation or re-setting of the Biblical words, this is an effective use of the material. Firstly, it connects the action taking place in contemporary Britain with the historical records of Israel, asserting the massive historical continuity of kingship. This is surely vital since a monarchical system depends for a large part of its legitimacy on a feeling of tradition, and on lineage in both the personal and national sense. This particular family line may not go back all those thousands of years (a delicate matter for a British monarchy that has survived the centuries by shifting the crown between families with unrest at each transition to a greater or lesser extent), but the idea of kingship itself does depend on a sense of long tradition. The account of Solomon being anointed king by the representatives of God does not attempt to argue that George II – or indeed Elizabeth II – is the lineal descendent of Solomon and heir to the throne of Israel, but it does invest monarchy with the authority of thousands of years of custom.

Secondly, the anthem uses its Biblical quotation to enact a subtle but dramatic shift between the first and second stanzas. The opening lines narrate a piece of history in the past tense, stating that Zadok and Nathan anointed Solomon, before recounting in the same tense that the people "rejoiced", several times. The repetition of the word "rejoiced", woven into Handel's glorious and bombastic music, shakes it loose from the grammatical moorings of its original sentence, and lets the singers and audience revel in the word itself. The idea of rejoicing is rather detached from the context from which it is being quoted, and made the subject of a rhapsody for an occasion of rejoicing. As the musical elaborations on this word carry the verse to its end, the two final words introduce the next verse: "and said". In the following setting of "God save the king" and "Long live the king" the singers are both recounting the words of the people in the Biblical quotation and wishing health and success to their own monarch being crowned. The resetting of the words in a coronation anthem telescopes the two time periods together, so that the singing of the quotation enacts the very celebration and acclamation it describe. The monarch is praised and blessed by the performance of the account of Solomon being praised and blessed. Particularly when performed by massed choir and orchestra, this can provide a powerful emotional effect which appears to abolish the historical gap between the time within the narrative and the time of the performers, mingling past and present in one highly-charged moment of ritual. This is, of course, exactly in line with the ideology that a coronation ceremony is intended to assert: the idea that centuries of historical time, and the authority they confer, are embodied in the person currently sitting on the throne.

As I mentioned above, this is not the ideology found throughout the Old Testament. The passage this anthem quotes is from 1 Kings, a book that is certainly in favour of Solomon's kingship, but the account of the beginnings of the Israelite monarchy given in the books of Samuel show a very different attitude to kings.

> Then all the elders of Israel gathered together and came to Samuel at Ramah, and said to him, "You are old and your sons do not follow in your ways; appoint for us, then, a king to govern us, like other nations." But the thing displeased Samuel . . . [and he] prayed to the LORD and the LORD said to Samuel, "Listen to the voice of the people in all they

say to you, for they have rejected me from being king over
them. . . . Now then, listen to their voice; only – you shall
solemnly warn them, and show them the ways of the king who
shall reign over them.

(1 Samuel 8:4-9)

Samuel's description of the tyranny of kings who will extort money
and supplies from them, take their children as soldiers and servants,
and impose slavery on the people ends with the dire warning "And
in that day you will cry out because of your king, whom you have
chosen for yourselves, but the LORD will not answer you in that
day" (1 Samuel 8:18). The initiation of the monarchy in Israel, which
will lead in a couple of generations to the anointing of Solomon, is
explicitly framed here as a rejection of God's rule, and a disastrous
turning away from divine authority and guidance. There are also pro-
monarchical strands in the Old Testament, but it is difficult to see the
collection as a ringing endorsement of kingship as an expression of
God's will and the people's best interests.

These state ceremonies use the Bible in distinctively different ways,
one involving a Bible as a symbol whose words are not spoken out
loud, whilst the other appropriates Biblical words and resets them
as part of a ceremony. As I have suggested, both these examples
can be criticised for their inconsistency with some significant part
of the actual contents of the Biblical books, though both also make
sophisticated and effective use of what they borrow. Reading them in
the modern context reveals a subtle use of the Bible to mean several
things that could not be exactly squared with a careful reading of the
texts. It is also fair to say that these appropriations or re-readings of
the Bible have some effect on the meanings generally attributed to
it in our culture. Perhaps no-one has ever regarded the presence of
the Bible in the inauguration ceremony as a definite statement about
congruence between the Constitution of the United States and the
Christian Scriptures, nor watched a British coronation on TV and
come away thinking that they've been misreading the Old Testament
kingship narratives for the last few years. Nonetheless, the association
between the state ceremonies and the Bible contributes to a general
sense that the Bible is on the side of authority. It frames the Bible as
a book that sits easily alongside power, and legitimates the existence
of rulers, hierarchies and elite groups in modern society. However
much Biblical scholars or left-wing Christian activists might disagree
with this account of the Bible, and however much the Bible informed

historical struggles for liberation such as the civil rights movement, it is still frequently seen as the natural companion of powerful people.[1] These uses of the Bible contribute to this general impression, acting as implicit "readings" of the meaning of the Biblical books which build up over time.

Shakespeare and the Acknowledged Legislators

Shakespeare is often used to support a point by supplying a telling phrase.[2] Lord Lea remarked in a debate on the presidency of the European Union in 2005 that

> My noble friend Lord Tomlinson does not like the idea of horse trading, so I will not call it that. It does not make much difference what we call it –as Shakespeare said, "A rose by any other name would smell as sweet".[3]

A similar use was made of Shakespeare's words by David Kidney in the previous year, when he ended his speech about supplying healthier food to schools with these words:

---

1. This is true of the political cultures of both Britain and the US, again in very different ways. The existence of a state church, which performs state ceremonies and some of whose bishops sit in the second chamber of the legislature, brings the Christian establishment close to the ruling classes of British society. The strong presence of religious language in US politics, to the extent that a presidential candidate would be instantly unelectable if they described themselves as an atheist, demonstrates a different but even stronger association between Christianity and political power.
2. I have deliberately limited my discussion below to moments when Members of Parliament explicitly mention Shakespeare's name when quoting his works. This will unfortunately exclude a lot of examples of quotation where both the speaker and the audience recognise that a Shakespearean reference is being made, but I wanted to rule out instances when politicians were simply using a turn of phrase that originated with Shakespeare but which has become part of the general rhetorical store of English public debate. Examples such as "more in sorrow than in anger", "the primrose path", whilst they are Shakespearean quotations in one sense, have become so detached from the author who first wrote them that it is doubtful how often people know that they are "quoting Shakespeare" when they employ these phrases. I wanted to focus on moments when speakers were deliberately employing Shakespeare for their own purposes, and the mention of his name seemed the best way to ensure that, even if it excluded other intriguing cases.
3. All the following quotations from remarks and speeches in the Houses of Parliament are from the Hansard online archive.

Shakespeare scholars may recall Julius Caesar's line: "Let me have men about me that are fat". Today, I call for the opposite: with apologies to the Bard's fans for my poor imitation of his prose, let me have people about me whose bellies hang not over their waistbands; exercise and balanced diet will keep them more years from the Grim Reaper's hands. I commend the Bill to the House.

There is very little that is particularly "Shakespearean" about these phrases. The words of another famous poet would do roughly the same job, as was demonstrated by the following exchange during a debate over age discrimination in employment:

Mr. Robinson: In the immortal words of the songwriter Tom Lehrer, however, the Bill would be "Full of sound and fury signifying absolutely nothing". I wonder whether, as legislators, we are in the business of trying to do that.

Mr. Forman: It was Shakespeare.

Mr. Robinson: I was thinking of Tom Lehrer, but I am reminded that I am quoting from Shakespeare.

As the confusion between the two great lyricists, Shakespeare and Lehrer, suggests, these speeches seem to be using Shakespeare mostly as the source of a well-turned aphorism. It is worth noting that in none of the cases above is the quotation particularly central to the point being made. In every quotation the point is made essentially separately and a Shakespearean tag is added to increase the force of the point. Indeed, in the example from the speech about school meals, the quotation was used to show that Shakespeare imagined a statesman wanting exactly the opposite, and David Kidney supplied a mock-Shakespearean phrase about those "whose bellies hang not over their waistbands" to make his point. There is little implication here that Shakespeare's wisdom is being drawn upon, or that his insight into human character is being put at the disposal of the Parliament to help them make the right decision. There is little in the notion of something being "full of sound and fury and signifying nothing" that connects it to the bill on age limits in job adverts, and no obvious association between the way a rose's name affects its scent and the topic of the European Union's presidency. The fact that Shakespeare is somewhat superfluous to the points being made (or even runs contrary to them) points to another aspect of these quotations. They are concerned with ways of arguing, not the subject being discussed. Similar quotations can be found in a local government finance debate, when Phil Hope suggested that "the lady doth protest too much" regarding Maurice Saatchi's complaints that the activities of the government around the proposed traffic congestion charge demonstrated "the insolence of office", or when Martin Smyth (inaccurately) ascribed to Shakespeare the idea that the "road to hell is paved with good intentions". Shakespeare's value here lies largely in its utility as a put-down, a way to criticise the way in which a debate is being carried out, rather than shed light on the topic being discussed.

There is also a broader sense that Shakespeare is being used as part of the general language game carried out in Parliament. Many of the quotations from Shakespeare that appear in debates seem less concerned with shedding light on the question being debated, or even the ways in which that debate is being carried out, than with bolstering the speaker's rhetorical self-presentation. A Shakespearean line tagged onto a point, particularly when it is advertised as such, is a cultural credential that suggests a certain level of education and authority in a speaker. It also signals that they are familiar with the cultural and linguistic world of a particular world; in this case, the world of predominantly white, upper-class, privately-educated men who constitute the British political class. This kind of Shakespearean reference marks a speaker as "one of us", not so much by presenting a dazzling image that casts the point being discussed in a radically new light, or by arguing from the authority of a much-respected historical author, but by discreetly presenting the credentials of a particular background, upbringing and social sphere. Most of the points being made with Shakespeare quotations in the Parliament archives could be equally well-supported by references to *Doctor Who* or *Gilmore Girls*, but using those works would send a different signal. Despite the fact that many people are well-versed in all three works, citing the latter two would mark membership of a very different cultural and social group.

Perhaps the most remarkable use of Shakespeare I have found in the recent archives of the British Parliament is in a speech made in the upper chamber by Lord McCarthy, whilst debating the Sexual Offences (Amendment) Bill in 2000. This proposed to lower the age of consent for homosexual sex to sixteen, bringing it in line with the equivalent age for heterosexual sex. McCarthy's speech, which argued in favour of the bill, ranged over various topics, including entrenched attitudes towards gay people, the protection of vulnerable young people, and the homosexual experiences that upper-class young men often accrued at exclusive schools and in elite army regiments. In summing up, he used Shakespearean theatre as a way to encourage his fellow lords to consider how their social attitudes might change, and how far those attitudes might have been founded on prejudice. It is worth quoting this section of the speech at some length:

> I have always found that one of the ways that I can purge my prejudices is to think of my past attitudes to Shakespeare. When I first saw *The Taming of the Shrew*, I sided with Petruchio. I cheered for Petruchio. I cannot now stand *The Taming of the Shrew*. I certainly cannot stand the last speech in *The Taming of the Shrew*. Petruchio was a sick sexist and should have been arrested. But I did not think that in 1948. I call that progress.
>
> I cannot remember when I first began to dislike the last act of *The Merchant of Venice*. There are nasty people in *The Merchant of Venice*. But I can remember the first time I felt what an insult, what a horror it was, when Antonio makes Shylock become a Christian. I did not think that many years ago.
>
> Finally, since we are talking about homosexuality, up until the 1960s, the actor who played Osric invariably played him as an effeminate ponce – what the actors called at the time a "ponce" part. He flipped around with his handkerchief all the time. If your Lordships are interested, there is on tape, eternally captured, Peter Cushing's wonderful example of the effeminate ponce in the Olivier film. Nobody would play it like that now. There is such a thing as progress. You just have to get there.

Lord McCarthy's speech uses controversial Shakespeare plays as a way of examining the shifts in social attitudes. It relies on his audience accepting as a given that of course *The Merchant of Venice* contains troublingly anti-Semitic characters and *The Taming of the Shrew* contains troublingly misogynist characters. His reminder that within his own theatregoing he can remember the entirely opposite view being generally acceptable implies that social attitudes can shift drastically within decades, and moral feelings that might have been formed in an earlier era must be scrutinised again. The character of Osric in theatrical tradition brings in gay people more explicitly once the main point has been established with more famously controversial characters, as *Hamlet* is hardly regarded as an "issue play" about homosexuality. This speech is unusual since it uses Shakespeare not as a mark of cultured identity, or the source of an apposite phrase, but as an example of how our deeply-felt reactions to human drama (in several senses) can be less fixed than we might think. The argument gains force from the fact that Shakespeare is regarded as authoritative and lasting; if even Shakespeare can apparently mean something entirely different when looked at in a different way, the speech implies, so can our sexual attitudes and ethics.

"You're entitled to anything, 'cos Shakespeare . . ."

"Comedy Tragedy History" by the British rap artist Akala provides a final example which points beyond the remit of this chapter. I have discussed non-literary and non-religious uses of Shakespeare so far, avoiding works like *Paradise Lost* which draw heavily on Biblical material, or *West Side Story* and other radical adaptations of Shakespeare. However, this record references Shakespeare in a way that differs from most other adaptations. Akala wrote the rap in half an hour, after being challenged on the radio station BBC 1Xtra to produce a piece that involved as many Shakespearean titles as possible. This challenge was the result of Akala's use of the title "the Black Shakespeare" to describe himself, and the first verse of the resulting work runs thus:

> Dat boy Akala's a diamond fella
> All you little boys are a Comedy of Errors
> You bellow but you fellows get played like the cello
> I'm doing my ting you're jealous like Othello
> Who you? What you gonna do?
> All you little boys get Tamed like the Shrew
> You're mid-summer dreamin'
> Your tunes ain't appealing
> I'm Capulet, you're Montague, I ain't feeling
> I am the Julius Caesar hear me
> The Merchant of Venice couldn't sell your CD
> As for me, All's Well That Ends Well
> Your boy's like Macbeth, you're going to Hell
> Measure for Measure, I am the best here
> You're Merry Wives of Windsor not King Lear
> I don't know about Timon
> I know he was in Athens
> When I come back like Hamlet you pay for your action

Akala's use of the play titles brings Shakespeare into the boasting style familiar from rap battling, making a point of his cultural literacy and his ability to handle the names of early modern works within and alongside the oral structures of rap. This first verse performs the same kind of verbal display as we saw earlier in the Shakespearean tags used by politicians, but to rather different effect. In the mouth of an Oxbridge-educated Member of Parliament, the Shakespearean references work to confirm the status that has already been conferred upon the speaker, asserting their connection with elite culture and power. As I suggested, it acts as a verbal marker of authority, continuing the association between Shakespeare and the right to be listened to respectfully. In the case of "Comedy Tragedy History", Akala works with the wide gap between the cultural status of Shakespeare and hip-hop, simultaneously asserting the value of his art form and playing with the juxtaposition of traditionally "high" culture with rapping. He claims the right to handle Shakespeare, remarking, "If you're entitled to Shakespeare, you're entitled to anything, 'cos Shakespeare is presented as the most high-brow, unattainable thing in the world" (in Hansen, 74).

At times it gestures to the plot or theme of the plays, such as the references to revenge tragedy in the *Hamlet* and the hell imagery in *Macbeth*, and at others it points up the disjunction between the titles and the context they appear in here. The jibes that "the Merchant of Venice couldn't sell your CD" and "you little boys are a Comedy of Errors" employ the names of venerated cultural artefacts in order to disrespect an imagined opponent, turning the titles of revered literary works into a quick punchline. In one sense this is remarkably apt, given the long arc Shakespeare's plays have travelled on the way to becoming regarded as paradigms of cultural value. As previous chapters showed, in Shakespeare's own lifetime plays were not watched or read as high culture, but as part of the entertainment industry of early modern London. They were first printed in flimsy quartos, reviled by religious and civic leaders, and performed in disreputable theatres where food and sex were also being sold. Banished from the respectable parts of the city, early modern theatre was regarded as potentially subversive of law and order, and the moral character of young people. Akala's appropriation of the titles of Shakespeare plays into his rap returns them to a popular form, whilst simultaneously marking how incongruous it might seem to declare "Measure for Measure, I am the best here/ You're Merry Wives of Windsor, I'm King Lear".

Hip-hop, a form that works by sampling and citing, quoting and reworking, is particularly suitable for this kind of ironic display. Throwing the names of Shakespeare plays around in a rapidly-composed rap foregrounds the centuries of history that stand between us and their original context, marking their distance and highlighting how far we are from appreciating them in the way their original audiences would. It demonstrates their oddness and strangeness, in their refusal to be easily adapted into this form. It also reveals the way Shakespeare's name is used to invoke cultural authority across all sorts of contexts in contemporary societies. Akala's overt cultural one-upmanship, mockingly using Shakespeare for improbable taunts, calls attention to the subtler and more apparently natural ways in which other people use Shakespeare to aggrandise themselves. He displays in ironic and heightened form the same processes that can be seen regularly in the words of speeches of politicians, judges and others in the public eye. "Comedy, Tragedy, History" alerts us to the fact that the apt quotation of *Hamlet* by a lawyer, or the reference in a news report to "star-crossed lovers", or the business seminar's mention of *Richard III*, are all part of a game that involves co-opting cultural authority. By performing the trick in clearer view of the audience, Akala simultaneously celebrates hip-hop's omnivorous capacity for cultural remixing, and points to the less noticeable uses of Shakespeare going on all around us.

Shakespeare, the Bible, and Beyond

In this chapter I have chosen a few examples of Shakespeare and the Bible being quoted, referred to or used in contexts that don't obviously involve religion or dramatic literature. As I mentioned earlier, this isn't an attempt to survey the range of contexts in which these texts are quoted in contemporary society (which would require a number of volumes to itself), nor to produce an over-arching theory about how citation and appropriation works. Instead, I wanted to examine some particular examples to show how apparently obvious or simple references to Shakespeare and the Bible can involve complex forms of appropriation and reworking. The seemingly natural use of a Bible during the inauguration, or the quotation of Shakespeare in Parliament, becomes much more incongruous and noticeable when they are examined in more depth. Nor does the incongruity of swearing an oath on a book that instructs people not to swear oaths, or celebrating a coronation with words from a work that is decidedly ambivalent about monarchs, mean that these uses are simply wrong or mistaken. As earlier chapters have demonstrated, there is no neutral, objective meaning that these texts contain, against which other uses can be checked and evaluated. Every use or quotation involves making meaning by drawing on the ideas and associations that surround Shakespeare and the Bible. In turn, they reflect back onto the texts, gradually building up contours of interpretation around them and contributing to the profile of these texts in our shared cultures. Thus citing Shakespeare or the Bible outside their expected contexts qualifies as a "reading" in both senses, drawing meaning out for a specific moment and in doing so shaping the general understanding of the text being quoted.

(After)Words of Power

In the introduction to this book I suggested it might help to make Shakespeare and the Bible look strange. Unlike many introductory works, which try to make the reader familiar with a topic they haven't had much contact with before, this book approaches a subject with which almost every reader will be familiar.[1] Surrounded by quotations, adaptations, references, adverts, jokes, polemics and speeches that originate with the collections of books we call "the Bible and Shakespeare", most readers will already have a strong idea of what these texts mean. Even if they have never opened a copy of either, most will have a broad sense of the significance of these works. This may include an appreciation of their religious and literary value, or simply the authority ascribed to them by others. For some they may represent the touchstones of a glorious cultural inheritance, whilst for others they may symbolise the abuse of power and the obscurantism of those who want to maintain that power. A large part of my task in this book has been to hold

---

1. One of the complaints frequently heard from expert scholars in both fields is that everyone outside their area of study – from colleagues in other disciplines, to radio presenters, to their lawyer – seems to think they're an expert in the subject. They have been known to grumble that marine biologists and tax accountants don't spend their time being told that they're wrong about the subject they've worked on for decades by someone who has read a newspaper editorial or heard an urban legend. Nor are they likely to have their honesty and integrity called into question by the adherents of conspiracy theories, which abound in both fields, and be accused of covering up the truth for their own selfish interests and financial benefit. Whilst this may be irksome from time to time, the general interest in the topics studied by those in Shakespeare Studies and Biblical Criticism is a mark of how seriously they are taken by our public culture. The (entirely correct) idea that everyone has a right to an opinion on these matters is ultimately a mark of the value placed upon them, and the role they continue to play in our shared social world.

the two sets of texts far enough away for us to catch a glimpse of them beyond the distorting lenses of our previous assumptions and experience. Those factors that have shaped our sense of the Bible and Shakespeare may not be wrong, but they have familiarised us to certain ways of reading, and made our engagement with these texts feel natural and inevitable.

Another task that falls to any book tackling Shakespeare and the Bible as "sacred texts" is to trace their parallel (and overlapping) but different trajectories. When people treat Shakespeare as Scripture, or the Bible as a literary classic, it can help us to appreciate what is going on if we know what Scripture or literary classics look like in other situations. To put it bluntly, when Gary Taylor – amongst many, many other critics – describes Shakespeare as "a secular Bible", that statement means a lot more if we have a solid understanding of what the non-secular Bible looks like. Likewise, some of my own scholarly work elsewhere has involved studying theologians and Biblical critics – such as Rowan Williams and N. T. Wright – who use Shakespeare as an analogy, and trying to clarify what they mean by "Shakespeare" in this context.

There are many people who place enormous value upon these texts, and organise their emotional, artistic and spiritual lives around them, or live their lives within communities shaped by traditions of interpretation that centre on these texts. We have seen in previous chapters the diversity of methods which are used to interpret the books in question, and the ways in which institutions validate themselves by reference to them. Part of that high valuation must involve a clear, or at least a definite, sense of what exactly the texts are, and how their authority can be understood. The histories of Shakespeare and the Bible can, in this sense, work as checks on each other, as control experiments to show what has happened when certain cultural and religious elements are or are not present in the reaction.

Devout Christians who regard the Bible both as inspired Scripture and as works of literary art can look at the history of Shakespeare to understand what sets the Biblical books and their interpretation apart from "merely" great literature. Shakespeare enthusiasts who find inspiration and wisdom in the works of the playwright might want to gain some appreciation of the way the Bible is used and understood, in order to distinguish their activities from religious reverence or even occult superstition. Those people who are deeply involved with either collections of texts should understand the history and use of the other, if not to revere theirs less, then perhaps to revere it better. They can appreciate more precisely the contours of its meaning, and prevent their respect from collapsing into a vague, non-specific sense that it is good and important and should not be slighted.

This effort to clarify the differences between the two collections of texts is made rather more complicated by their connected histories. They are connected via influence: Shakespeare lived in a culture saturated with religion and religious controversy, in an era when the reading of the Bible was a major political issue. When he entitles a play *Measure for Measure*, he borrows from the promise (or warning) in the seventh chapter of Matthew that "with the measure you use, it will be measured to you". More elaborately, when Bottom in *A Midsummer Night's Dream* declares that "The eye of man hath not heard, the ear of man hath not seen, man's hand is not able to taste, his tongue to conceive, nor his heart to report what my dream was", he provides a jumbled echo of the first letter to the Corinthians, with its declaration that the eye has not seen and the ear has not heard what God has prepared. As Shakespeare's reputation grew and his works became a cultural touchstone, the process took place within a literary tradition in which the Bible still played a very large part. Perhaps the highest point of rhetoric in praise of Shakespeare was reached in the Victorian era, when Evangelical Protestantism had become the dominant influence on public culture, with a strong emphasis on Bible reading as one of its major tenets. In the last year of that era, when George Bernard Shaw was searching for a term to disparage the over-enthusiastic honour and glory lavished on the playwright, he instinctively reached for a religious pun, calling it "Bardolatry".

Thus Shakespeare's influence was shaped and channelled by existing understandings of what a "sacred text" looked and sounded like, and was exerted alongside that of the Bible. As I suggested in the introduction, the categories that John Barton has developed to describe and explain the operations of the Bible as a holy book map surprisingly easily onto certain ways in which Shakespeare is used, interpreted and revered. We may be able to cross-check between the history of Shakespeare and that of the Bible in English-speaking cultures, but we will not be able to entirely separate their trajectories or influences. However, this needn't detract from the usefulness of studying them alongside each other; tracing their interrelations is itself valuable and can teach us a great deal about the histories that shaped the books we have today.

This book has developed a trajectory from more historical and factual material about the collections of texts that are referred to as "Shakespeare and the Bible" towards more open-ended and interpretative surveys of the ways in which they are used and quoted in contemporary culture. The chapters on canonical issues and textual criticism cover subjects which most readers of either the Bible or the works of Shakespeare will not need to consider from day to day, though they have undoubtedly shaped the form in which these texts are sold and the ways they are read. The later chapters on citations and the institutions that validate themselves by reference to the texts are more likely to have an immediate application. The analytical work whose results are presented by the early chapters can generally only be carried out with a high level of specialised education, coupled with expensive libraries, substantial support from international institutions and other scarce resources. This means that relatively few readers of this book will be carrying out their own research that traces the same path of textual and historical scholarship in order to contest or disagree with those conclusions individually, though they may certainly want to incorporate into their own reading life the insights that previous research has provided. The later chapters give examples of "readings" that almost everyone who reads this book will be able to do for themselves: recognising a quotation, looking sceptically at the mission statement of a college, asking themselves for what purpose a Bible verse is being used in a politician's speech. I hope that this book stimulates a host of "readings" in all sorts of forms, with the strangeness of the past aiding a recognition of the present's own remarkable strangeness.

Bibliography and Further Reading

Bibliography

Akala, "Comedy Tragedy History" (Illa State, 2007)

Augustine of Hippo, *Confessions*, tr. R.S. Pine-Coffin (London: Penguin, 1961)

Barton, J., *The Spirit and the Letter: Studies in the Biblical Canon* (London: SPCK, 1997)

Barr, J., *Fundamentalism* (London: SCM, 1977)

Bloom, A., *The Closing of the American Mind: How Higher Education Has Failed Democracy and Impoverished the Souls of Today's Students.* (New York, Simon and Schuster, 1987)

Bloom, H., *Shakespeare: The Invention of the Human* (London: Fourth Estate, 2008)

The Book of Common Prayer (Cambridge: cum privilegio)

Braaten, C.E. and Jenson, R.W., eds., *Reclaiming the Bible for the Church* (Edinburgh: T & T Clark, 1995)

Bradley, A.C., *Shakespearean Tragedy: Lectures on Hamlet, Othello, King Lear, Macbeth* 2nd ed. (London: Macmillan, 1905)

Brooks, C., *The Well-Wrought Urn: Studies in the Structure of Poetry* (London: Harcourt Brace, 1947)

Bruce, F.F., *The New Testament Documents: Are They Reliable?* (Indiana: InterVarsity Press, repr. 1982)

Chapman, M., *Doing Anglican Theology* (London: T & T Clark, 2012) [unpaginated ebook]

Davies, P., *Whose Bible Is It Anyway?* (London: T & T Clark, 1995)

Dawson, A., "The Imaginary Text, or the Curse of the Folio" in Barbara Hodgdon and W.B. Worthen, eds., *A Companion to Shakespeare and Performance* (Oxford: Blackwell, 2005) pp. 141-161

Donfried, K.P., *Who Owns the Bible?: Towards the Recovery of a Christian Hermeneutic* (New York: Herder and Herder, 2006)

Dunn, J. and McKnight, S., eds., *The Historical Jesus in Recent Research* (Winona Lake: Eisenbrauns, 2005)

Ehrman, B.D., *The Bible: A Literary and Historical Introduction* (Oxford: Oxford University Press, 2013)

Elliott, K. and Moir, I., *Manuscripts and the Text of the New Testament: An Introduction for English Readers* (Edinburgh: T & T Clark, 1995)

Evangelical Alliance, "About Us" [www.eauk.org/connect/about-us]

Ford, D.F. and Stanton, G., eds., *Reading Texts, Seeking Wisdom: Scripture and Theology* (London: SCM, 2003)

Gilmour, R., *The Victorian Period: The Intellectual and Cultural Context of English Literature, 1830-1890* (Middlesex: Longman, 1993)

Grant, R. and Tracey, D., *A Short History of the Interpretation of the Bible*, 2nd ed. (Philadelphia: Fortress, 1984)

Greenblatt, S., *Shakespearean Negotiations: The Circulation of Social Energy in Renaissance England* (Berkeley and Los Angeles: University of California Press, 1988)

Grudem, W., Collins, C.J. and Schreiner, T.R., eds., *Understanding Scripture: An Overview of the Bible's Origin, Reliability, and Meaning* (Wheaton, Illinois: Crossway, 2012) [unpaginated ebook]

Hansard 1803-2005, UK Parliament [http://hansard.millbanksystems.com]

Hansen, A., *Shakespeare and Popular Music* (London: Continuum, 2010)

Holloway, P., 'Letter to the Editor: Honorary degrees to bring a little less honor', *The Sewanee Purple*, 6th Feb 2015 [http://thesewaneepurple.org/2015/02/06/letter-to-the-editor-honorary-degrees-to-bring-a-little-less-honor]

Irenaeus of Lyons, *The Writings of Irenaeus*, tr. Alexander Roberts and W.H. Rambaut (Edinburgh, T & T Clark, repr. Aeterna Press, 2015)

Johnson, S., *Johnson on Shakespeare*, ed. Walter Raleigh (London: Henry Prowse, 1908)

Jowett, J., *Shakespeare and Text* (Oxford: Oxford University Press, 2007)

King, J.N., ed., *Voices of the English Reformation: A Sourcebook* (Philadelphia: University of Pennsylvania Press, 2004)

Knights, L.C., *Explorations: Essays in Criticism Mainly on the Literature of the Seventeenth Century* (London: Chatto and Windus, 1946)

Lamb, C., *Selected Prose*, ed. Adam Philips (London: Penguin, 1985) van Liere, F., *An Introduction to the Medieval Bible* (Cambridge: Cambridge University Press, 2014)

Makaryk, I.R., ed., *Encyclopedia of Contemporary Literary Theory: Approaches, Scholars, Terms* (University of Toronto Press, 1993, repr. 2000)

Manguel, A., *A History of Reading* (London: HarperCollins, 1996)

Marcus, L., *Unediting the Renaissance: Shakespeare, Marlowe, Milton* (London: Routledge, 1996)

Marsden, J.I., *The Re-Imagined Text*: *Shakespeare, Adaptation and Eighteenth-Century Literary Theory* (Lexington: University of Kentucky Press, 1995)

Marowitz, C., *Recycling Shakespeare* (London: Applause Books, 1991)

Massie, A., "We Can't Cast Away Our Bible", *The Telegraph*, 11th August 2013 [http://blogs.telegraph.co.uk/culture/allanmassie/100070349/we-cant-cast-away-our-bible]

McDonald, R., ed., *Shakespeare: An Anthology of Criticism and Theory 1945-2000* (Oxford: Blackwell, 2004)

McDonald, L.M., *The Biblical Canon: Its Origin, Transmission and Authority* (Peabody, Massachusetts: Hendrickson, 2007)

Metzger, B. and Ehrman, B., *The Text of the New Testament: Its Transmission, Corruption and Restoration* (Oxford: Oxford University Press, 2005)

Morgan, R. and Barton, J., *Biblical Interpretation* (Oxford: Oxford University Press, 1988)

Mulryne, J.R. and Shewring, M., eds., *Shakespeare's Globe Rebuilt* (Cambridge: Cambridge University Press, 1997)

National Theatre, "Timon of Athens" [http://www.nationaltheatre.org.uk/shows/timon-of-athens]. Accessed 9th May 2014.

No Fear Shakespeare, *Hamlet* (SparkNotes) [nfs.sparknotes.com/hamlet]

Ong, W.J., *Orality and Literacy: Technologizing the Word* (London: Routledge, 1982, repr. 2002)

Parker, D.C., *Textual Scholarship and the Making of the New Testament* (Oxford: Oxford University Press, 2012)

Pollard, T., ed., *Shakespeare's Theater: A Sourcebook* (Oxford: Blackwell, 2004)

Richardson, C., *Early Christian Fathers* (Phildelphia: Westminster Press, 1953, repr. 1995)

Shapiro, J., *Contested Will: Who Wrote Shakespeare?* (London: Faber and Faber, 2011)

Sidney, P., *The Major Works*, ed. Katherine Duncan-Jones (Oxford: Oxford University Press, 1989, repr. 2002)

Shakespeare's Globe, "About Us" [http://www.shakespearesglobe.com/about-us]

Spurgeon, C., *Shakespeare's Imagery and What It Tells Us* (Cambridge: Cambridge University Press, 1935)

Stern, T., "The Forgery of Some Modern Author?: Theobald's Shakespeare and Cardenio's Double Falsehood", *Shakespeare Quarterly,* Volume 62, Number 4, Winter 2011, pp. 555-593

Styan, J.L., *The Shakespeare Revolution* (Cambridge University Press, repr. 1983)

Taylor, G., *Reinventing Shakespeare: A Cultural History from the Restoration to the Present* (London: Vintage, 1991)

Thomassen, E., ed., *Canon and Canonicity: The Formation and Use of Scripture* (Copenhagen: Museum Tusculum Press, 2010)

Tucker, P., *Secrets of Acting Shakespeare* (London: Routledge, 2002)

Wax, T., "Trevin Wax Interviews N.T. Wright", *The Gospel Coalition*, 9th Nov 2007 [http://blogs.thegospelcoalition.org/trevinwax/2007/11/19/trevin-wax-interview-with-nt-wright-full-transcript]

Weingust, D., *Acting from Shakespeare's First Folio: Theory, Text and Performance* (London: Routledge, 2006)

Wiles, M., *Explorations in Theology 4* (London: SCM, 1979)

Williams, R., "Historical Criticism and Sacred Text", in David F. Ford and Graham Stanton, eds., *Reading Texts, Seeking Wisdom: Scripture and Theology* (London: SCM, 2003) pp. 217-244

Yachnin, P. and Slights, J., eds., *Shakespeare and Character: Theatre, History, Performance and Theatrical Persons* (Basingstoke: Palgrave Macmillan, 2009)

Further Reading

Aland, K. and Aland, B., *The Text of the New Testament*, tr. Erroll F. Rhodes, 2nd ed. (Grand Rapids: Eerdmans, 1989)

Armstrong, K., *The Bible: The Biography* (New York: Atlantic Books, 2007)

Barton, J., *Holy Writings, Sacred Text: The Canon in Early Christianity* (Louisville: Westminster John Knox, 1997)

— *The Nature of Biblical Criticism* (Louisville: Westminster John Knox, 2007)

— *What Is The Bible?* 3rd ed. (London: SPCK, 2009)

Bate, J., *The Soul of the Age: the Life, Mind and World of Shakespeare* (London: Viking, 2009)

Bradbrook, M.C., *Shakespeare: The Poet in his World* (London: Routledge, repr. 2003)

Beauman, S., *The Royal Shakespeare Company: A History of Ten Decades* (Oxford: Oxford University Press, 1982)

Callaghan, D., *Shakespeare Without Women* (London: Routledge, 1999)

Carson, C. and Karim-Cooper, F., eds., *Shakespeare's Globe: A Theatrical Experiment* (Cambridge: Cambridge University Press, 2008)

Dobson, M., *The Making of the National Poet* (Oxford: Clarendon, 1992)

Duncan-Jones, K., *Shakespeare: An Ungentle Life* (London: Arden, 2014)

Ehrman, B.D. and Wallace, D.B., *The Reliability of the New Testament* (Minneapolis: Fortress, 2011)

Howard, J.E., *Marxist Shakespeares* (London: Routledge, 2001)

Maguire, L., *Where There's a Will There's a Way* (London: Nicholas Brealey, 2011)

McLuskie, K. and Rumbold, K., *Cultural Value in Twenty-First Century England: The Case of Shakespeare* (Manchester: Manchester University Press, 2014)

Metzger, B., *The Canon of the New Testament: Its Origin, Development and Significance* (Oxford: Oxford University Press, 1997)

Moule, C.F.D., *The Birth of the New Testament* 3rd ed. (London: Continuum, 1981, repr. 2002)

Murphy, A., *A Concise Companion to Shakespeare and Text* (Oxford: Blackwell, 2007)

O'Connor, J., *Shakespearean Afterlives: Ten Characters With A Life Of Their Own* (London: Icon Books, 2005)

Pixley, J. and Boff, C., *The Bible, the Church and the Poor* (Maryknoll, NY: Orbis, 1990)

Riches, J., *The Bible: A Very Short Introduction* (Oxford: Oxford University Press, 2000)

Rogerson, J.W., *An Introduction to the Bible* (London: Penguin, 1999)

Sanders, E.P., *The Historical Figure of Jesus* (London: Penguin, 1993)

Sanders, J.A., *Canon and Community: A Guide to Canonical Criticism* (New York: Wipf and Stock, repr. 2000)

Smith, E., *The Cambridge Introduction to Shakespeare* (Cambridge: Cambridge University Press, 2007)

Stern, T., *Making Shakespeare: From Page to Stage* (London: Routledge, 2004)

Sturgess, K.C., *Shakespeare and the American Nation* (Cambridge: Cambridge University Press, 2004)

Taylor, G., *Reinventing Shakespeare* (London: Vintage, 1989)

Theissen, G., *The New Testament: History, Literature, Religion* (London: Continuum, 2003)

Werner, S., *Shakespeare and Feminist Performance: Ideology on Stage* (London: Routledge, 2005)

Williams, R., *Meeting God in Mark* (London: SPCK, 2014)

Index

You may also be interested in

The Bible as Literature
T.R. Henn

ISBN: 978 0 7188 3091 5

Tom Henn's classic work represents an important and illuminating reading for the student of English literature and religion, the general reader of the Bible and the Bible lover.

Based on the King James (Authorised) Version of the Bible, Dr Henn looks critically at the epic, narrative, lyric and dramatic qualities of the sacred texts. He examines the Bible's unique "forge of style" and the imagery which so profoundly gives the Bible its character. The Bible's immense variety, its capacity to speak to the heart and mind of the reader, its powerful readability and above all its sense of the eternal, are all brought into Henn's masterly work.

As Henn says: "The Bible has been burned deeply into the fabric of the life and literature of the English-speaking peoples. Its proverbs and its parables, its episodes sacred or profane, have been expounded in drama and poetry from the earliest written English."

Available now with more excellent titles in Paperback, Hardback, PDF and ePub formats from The Lutterworth Press

www.lutterworth.com

You may also be interested in

The Virtues and Vices in the Arts
A Sourcebook
Shawn R. Tucker

ISBN: 978 0 7188 9404 7
PDF: 978 0 7188 4410 3

The seven deadly sins are pride, envy, anger, sloth, gluttony, greed, and lust. The seven virtues are prudence, fortitude, temperance, justice, faith, hope, and love. *The Virtues and Vices in the Arts* brings all of them together and for the first time lays out their history in a collection of the most important philosophical, religious, literary, and art-historical works.

Starting with the Greco-Roman and Judeo-Christian antecedents, this anthology of source documents traces the tradition of virtues and vices through its cultural apex during the medieval era and then into their continued development and transformation from the Renaissance to the present. This anthology includes excerpts of Plato's *Republic*, the Bible, Dante's *Purgatorio*, and the writings of Friedrich Nietzsche and C.S. Lewis. Also included are works of art from medieval manuscripts; paintings by Giotto, Veronese, and Paul Cadmus; prints by Brueghel; and a photograph by Oscar Rejlander. What these works show is the vitality and richness of the virtues and vices in the arts from their origins to the present.

Available now with more excellent titles in Paperback, Hardback, PDF and ePub formats from The Lutterworth Press

www.lutterworth.com